Basic Comprehension Passages

Contents

Introduction		2
How to use this material		4
Section 1	Comprehension passages	6
Section 2	Cloze practice	96
Section 3	Vocabulary activities	104
Section 4	Dictation passages	117
Key		121

Longman

Introduction

The material in this book is for comprehension practice and related language work at an early post-elementary level. A significant feature of the book is that the reading texts are at a much higher level than the related exploitation.

The book is divided into four sections.

Section 1

This consists of thirty units, each of which is made up of a text with exercises for oral and written work. The following points should be noted:

THE TEXTS These are mainly narrative, with a few in the form of letters and diary extracts (partly for variety, partly for linguistic reasons). Although the language of the texts has not been significantly controlled, some structural items have been excluded. The main ones are certain tenses (Past Perfect, Present Perfect Progressive and Past Perfect Progressive), passives and certain conditional types.

THE EXPLOITATION This has been phased as follows:
Stage 1: Units 1–10 The emphasis here is on receptive skills. Comprehension practice consists, typically, of multiple choice practice, right/wrong statements, putting sentences in order to form a chronological sequence and, occasionally, some *yes/no* questions.
Stage 2: Units 11–20 Here the emphasis begins to shift to productive activities. Accordingly, the amount of multiple choice practice is decreased (together with other activities typical of the first stage) and the students now have to respond to a wider range of questions on the text (mainly of the *yes/no* type).
Stage 3: Units 21–30 Here the emphasis is on productive activities, which include batteries of mixed *wh-* and *yes/no* type questions, 'disguised' *wh*-questions (in the form of statements which the students have to reformulate as questions) and completion exercises.

It is intended that this phased approach should build up the students' confidence in coping with a text beyond their productive ability – which is something that many students have to be *persuaded* that they can do. *For this reason the students will only get the maximum value from this material if it is used in the order in which it is presented, stage by stage.* The range of exercise types is also intended to give the students confidence through familiarity, while being sufficiently varied to avoid monotony. Throughout the units in Section 1 there are also a number of constant features. They are:
Read and decide This is an introductory skim or scan activity, designed to get the students to do a quick initial reading of the text (and of course to provide them with a *reason* for reading).

Choose the right meaning This is an introductory vocabulary activity to focus attention on certain key lexical items in the text which might, at this level, interfere unduly with comprehension. It is designed as a learning rather than testing activity, and attention is always focussed on the context in which the item is used.

From Unit 21 onwards the students are asked to guess the meaning of selected items (an activity which can of course be introduced at an earlier level).

Guided composition For Units 1–20 this is usually a simple fill-in activity (words, phrases or clauses), often involving little more than using appropriate items from the text. The tasks at the third stage are designed to be a little more challenging and require the students to contribute bigger chunks of text or build up a short composition from notes.

Vocabulary practice This is a sentence completion exercise which recycles 10–12 vocabulary items from the text in a new context. Together with Section 3 it is intended to help build up progressively the students' mastery of key vocabulary used in the book.

Discussion The main purpose of this activity is to get the students to relate what they have read to their own experience. The questions should be modified or extended according to the needs and interests of the students. The students are also sometimes asked to suggest an ending for the story.

Most units also contain a 'reference' type activity, which asks the students to identify items in the text which are referred to through a pronominal form. The purpose is to get the students to look across sentence boundaries while they are reading. The sentences used in these exercises have either been taken from the text (see Unit 1C) or have been written about items in the text (see Unit 6C).

Section 2 Cloze practice

This consists of thirty extracts from the texts in Section 1 (i.e. one from each text), from which certain key grammatical features (tense forms, articles, prepositions and pronouns) have been omitted. In addition, some extracts are of the 'open' cloze type, with a variety of key words omitted (usually not more than one per sentence).

Section 3 Vocabulary activities

Here there is a set of exercises for each text in Section 1, with a consolidation battery after every fifth unit.

The aim of this section is to reactivate and reinforce key items of vocabulary (including, importantly, irregular past tense forms, prepositions and phrasal verbs) so as to ensure that the students are progressively mastering key vocabulary items in each text. It is felt that significantly increasing the students' vocabulary can and should be one of the major gains of using a book of this kind.

Section 4 Dictation passages

This section consists of fifteen short dictation passages which have been based on one or (more usually) two of the texts in Section 1. The point at which each dictation passage can be used is indicated in brackets after each text.

Note that material in Sections 2–4 should be done a week or so after the related unit has been completed.

Key

This provides the 'answers' to selected exercises in Section 1. The aim has been to make the key as comprehensive as possible (for reasons of space it cannot be complete!) both to clear up doubts and of course to save 'teacher time'.

You should note that the 'answers' to the guided compositions (especially in the later stages) and to some extent to the completion exercises (from Unit 21 onwards) are *suggestions* only. The alternative versions which the students are likely to produce should always be treated with interest and respect.

How to use this material

The following approach may be used:

1 *Set a reading goal.* Use the *Read and decide* activity for this purpose (unless you prefer an alternative activity of your own) to get the students to read the text quickly and silently. Set an appropriate time limit (e.g. 2–3 minutes or slightly longer if the text is likely to prove difficult).
2 *Establish background.* Get the students to give their own ideas about the people in the story e.g. as appropriate, their names, ages, appearance etc. This kind of speculation will help to bring the situation alive.
3 *Deal with key vocabulary.* Exercise A is intended for this purpose. If the students work in pairs for this activity, they will not only have to read the text again but also make their own decisions about the meaning of items with which they are not familiar. Stress that they must always look carefully at the context. Go through the exercise with the whole class.
4 *Ask the students to read the text again, this time more carefully, and to find the answers to the multiple choice questions in B.* The students should work individually for this activity (although they can compare answers). Go through the exercise with the whole class.
Note: after Unit 20, use any suitable exercise in place of B.

5 *Do any 'reference' exercises with the class.* Make sure that the students understand that the ability to identify pronominal references is an important part of efficient reading.
6 *Do other text-related exercises orally or in writing according to the needs of the class and the type of activity.* You may follow this general guide:

	Oral	Written
Stage 1	Make true statements Right or wrong?	Put these sentences in order
Stage 2	Answer these questions	Match the statements Complete this table
Stage 3	Answer these questions	Complete these sentences

7 *Get the students to react to the text.* In addition to the questions in the *Discussion* section, you may also ask the students to:
 – suggest a title for the text;
 – suggest a continuation for the story;
 – comment on things that happened in the story (e.g. to say whether they think that X did something right, silly, clever etc).
8 *Set homework.* It is assumed that the *Guided composition* and *Vocabulary practice* activities will be used mainly for this purpose, although the latter will also be found useful as a fill-in activity towards the end of the lesson. You should note that some guided composition activities at Stage 3 may require preparation with the class.
9 *Do other activities as required.* Both *Cloze practice* and *Vocabulary activities* should be done a week or so after the related unit has been completed. Both are suitable for pairwork in class and for the most part can be corrected by the students themselves. Some of the activities in the consolidation batteries (after every fifth unit in the *Vocabulary activities*) can be used for team games. The relevant dictation passage can then be used for final consolidation.

Section 1   Comprehension passages

1

> **Read and decide.**   Who found the boys? a) their father b) a policeman c) a friend

The two boys walked slowly across the valley. Then suddenly Fred stopped and sat down on a large stone. "It's no use," he said. "I can't go any further. I'm absolutely exhausted!"

George looked at him for a minute. "Oh come on!" he said. "It's not very
5 far now. Only five or six miles at the most."

"Yes, but it's uphill most of the way," Fred said. He pointed to the path in front of them. It went straight up the side of the valley. George sat down too. For a while the two boys said nothing. Then Fred pointed to some trees about half a mile ahead.

10 "There's a hut among those trees," he said. "Perhaps we can spend the night there."

"I'll go and take a look," George said. He ran down the path towards the hut and vanished among the trees. Fred followed more slowly.

"What's it like inside?" he asked when he reached the hut.

15 "Not bad," George called back. "It feels a little damp, but there's some wood in one corner, so we can light a fire."

The two boys cleaned out the hut and lit a fire. Then they had supper. They were both tired and they did not talk much. Before they went to bed, they put plenty of wood on the fire. George fell asleep almost at once, but Fred
20 lay awake for a long time, watching the flames. Then he too fell asleep.

Suddenly he was awake again. The fire was nearly out. He could hear noises outside. It sounded like voices. He woke up George.

"It's only the wind," he grumbled. "Go to sleep again!"

But it wasn't the wind! The voices came nearer until they were just outside
25 the hut. The door opened and a light shone on their faces. "They're here!" a voice called out. A policeman was standing in the doorway. He addressed the two boys. "You've given us a lot of trouble," he said. "We've looked all over the valley for you two!"

A   Find these words in the text:

exhausted (*line 3*); straight (*line 7*); ahead (*line 9*); hut (*line 10*); damp (*line 15*); addressed (*line 26*).

Now choose the right meaning.
1 small house
2 directly
3 very tired
4 spoke to
5 in front
6 wet

B   Choose the right answer.
1 Fred wanted to stop, but George wanted to: a) go back b) go on c) talk
2 The path in front of them was: a) long b) easy c) difficult
3 The boys lit a fire because: a) they could not see b) the hut was damp c) they wanted to cook
4 After supper, the boys: a) went to bed b) sat and talked c) cleaned out the hut
5 Fred woke up because: a) he heard a noise b) he was afraid c) he was cold
6 The policeman who came to the hut: a) wanted to sleep there b) was looking for the boys c) wanted to catch the boys

C   What do the words in italics refer to?
1 *He* pointed to the path in front of *them*.
2 Perhaps we can spend the night *there*.
3 *It* feels a little damp.
4 "*It*'s only the wind," *he* grumbled.
5 "*They*'re here," a voice called out.

D   Make true sentences.

Fred George	was very tired. wanted to go on. saw a hut among the trees. ran to the hut. went into the hut first. fell asleep quickly.	1 2 3 4 5 6

E   Put these sentences in the correct order.
1 The boys did not talk much.
2 The boys cleaned the hut out.
3 Fred watched the flames for a long time.
4 The boys went to bed.
5 Fred fell asleep.
6 The boys found a hut among the trees.
7 The boys had supper.

8 George fell asleep quickly.
9 The boys lit a fire.
10 The boys put plenty of wood on the fire.

F Guided composition. Use the sentences in E to complete this paragraph.

The boys . . . . They . . . it . . . and . . . . Then . . . .
They . . . because they were tired. After supper, . . . and . . . .
George . . . but Fred . . . . Then he . . . too.

G Vocabulary practice. Complete these sentences, using the words in the box.

| absolutely | at the most | damp | hut | path | valley |
| ahead | awake | exhausted | noise | straight | |

1 We lay . . . for a long time, listening to the . . . of the wind.
2 Most of the rooms were warm and dry, but my room felt a little . . . .
3 There's a small town not very far . . . . It's only two or three miles away . . . .
4 Follow this . . . through the trees. It goes . . . to the village.
5 Is that a house on the other side of the . . . ? No, it's too small. It's probably a . . . .
6 I went to bed early last night. I was . . . . !

H Discussion

Have you ever stayed away from home like this? (Why? What happened?)
Suggest an ending for this story.

2

> **Read and decide.** Did Jack and his friend get any fish for supper?

We were standing on the bridge, trying to catch some fish for supper when a small red plane flew almost directly above our heads. We could even see the pilot's face. "What on earth is he up to?" I asked. I felt rather annoyed.

"I think he's in trouble," Jack said. "His engine is making a strange noise."

"Well, *we* can't do anything, can we?" I said. "We can't even phone from here." We were on a boating holiday and we were miles from the nearest town.

"We can follow the plane down the river," Jack said. "Come on! Let's go!" I must admit I liked the idea. There weren't many fish in that part of the river and I was bored. We dropped our fishing lines and ran towards our boat. It lay under some bushes about a hundred yards down the river. Luckily the engine started almost at once and soon we were roaring down the river.

"But can the pilot land here?" I asked Jack. He came to this part of the country for a holiday almost every year and he knew the area well.

"There's a lake about fifteen miles down the river," Jack said. "If the pilot really is in trouble, he'll probably try to land there."

The river was already becoming wider. We went round a bend and there was the lake in front of us.

"Can you see anything?" Jack asked.

I looked across the lake. "No, absolutely nothing," I replied. "Wait a minute, though. There's something in the water, near that island in the middle." It was the small red plane!

We raced across the lake. By the time we reached the island, the pilot – a very young woman! – was sitting on top of the plane.

"Hi!" she called out to us. "Thanks for coming to help me. I'm sorry I disturbed you while you were fishing. Anyway, would you like some fish for supper?"

She reached into the plane and pulled out a large fish. "There's plenty more in here!" she said, laughing.

A Find these words and phrases in the text:

What . . . is he up to? (*line 3*); in trouble (*line 4*); bored (*line 10*); wider (*line 17*); bend (*line 17*); raced (*line 23*); disturbed (*line 26*).

Now choose the right meaning.
1. bigger
2. went quickly
3. What is he trying to do?
4. interrupted
5. not interested
6. (the river was) not straight
7. having difficulties

B Choose the right answer.

1. When the plane flew over their heads, Jack and his friend were: a) having supper b) fishing c) doing nothing
2. Jack said, "I think the pilot's in trouble" because: a) the plane was making a strange noise b) they could see the pilot's face c) the plane was very low
3. Jack knew the area well because: a) he had a boat b) he often came there c) he lived there
4. They saw the plane in the middle of: a) the lake b) the island c) the trees
5. When they reached the island, the pilot: a) was fishing b) was waiting for them c) was swimming

C What do the words in italics refer to?

1. *It* lay under some bushes.
2. "*He*'ll probably try to land *there*."
3. *It* was the small red plane.
4. "There's plenty more in *here*!"

D Right or wrong?

1. The pilot was a friend of Jack's.
2. Jack's friend did not want to go down the river.
3. Jack and his friend had a fast boat.
4. The river went into a lake.
5. Jack saw the red plane first.
6. Jack and his friend did not want to help the pilot.
7. Jack and his friend got a lot of fish for supper.

E Put these sentences in the correct order.

1. The engine was making a strange noise.
2. Jack and his friend found the plane in the middle of the lake.
3. Jack and his friend were fishing.
4. The pilot was safe.
5. Jack and his friend went down the river in their boat.
6. Jack and his friend decided to follow the plane.
7. Jack and his friend came to a lake.
8. A plane flew over their heads.

F Guided composition. Use the sentences in E to complete this paragraph.

Jack and his friend were on a boating holiday. One day, while . . . , a plane . . . . The engine . . . , so . . . . They . . . until . . . . There they . . . . The pilot . . . .

G Vocabulary practice. Complete these sentences, using the words in the box.

admit	bend	directly	flew	island	wider
area	bored	disturb	holiday	noise	

1 I'm sorry I made a lot of . . . last night. I hope I didn't . . . you.
2 This is the first week of our . . . , so we don't know the . . . very well yet.
3 What shall we do? Have you any ideas? I must . . . I'm feeling . . . !
4 The valley is just round this . . . . You'll see it in a minute when the path gets . . . .
5 The house was on an . . . , in the middle of a lake, and we . . . almost . . . over it.

H Discussion

The pilot was in trouble and Jack and his friend helped her. Have you ever helped anyone like this? Have you ever been in trouble like this? (For example, in a boat?)

11

3

> **Read and decide.** Who started the fire? a) a fireman b) Elsa's father c) someone in the crowd

They could see the smoke from the end of the street.

"It's *our* house!" Elsa shouted.

"It can't be," Alan said. But he knew that Elsa was right and they both began to run.

There was a small crowd in the street outside their house. Smoke was coming out of the front window of the downstairs room, but there was no sign of any flames.

And there was no sign of old Mr Cox, Elsa's father. He lived with them and had a room upstairs at the back of the house. He was not among the people in the crowd.

"Alan!" his wife shouted. "He's asleep upstairs! He probably went to bed and left the fire on in the front room!"

Her husband began to push his way through the crowd towards the front door.

"Don't be a fool!" someone shouted. "Wait for the firemen. They'll be here any minute."

But Alan knew that he must not wait. He put a handkerchief over his face and ran up the stairs. He pushed open the door of his father-in-law's room. Old Mr Cox was sleeping peacefully.

"What's the matter?" he cried as he woke up.

"Nothing to worry about. Just a small fire downstairs," Alan told him. "Now, get a coat on and put a handkerchief over your face like this."

At the top of the stairs Alan made old Mr Cox climb onto his back. Then he put a handkerchief over his own face and went down the stairs as quickly as he could. There was a cheer from the crowd as he came out of the house.

The fire engine and an ambulance arrived more or less at that moment. The first flames were just beginning to come out of the front window. "It's all my fault!" moaned old Mr Cox as they carried him into the ambulance. "I was reading the newspaper and I left it near the electric fire."

A Find these words and phrases in the text:

there was no sign of (*lines 6–7*); any minute (*line 16*); stairs (*line 18*); peacefully (*line 19*); a cheer (*line 25*); ambulance (*line 26*).

Now choose the right meaning.

1 a shout of happiness
2 they couldn't see (him)
3 very soon
4 a car to take people to hospital
5 quietly
6 steps inside the house

B Choose the right answer.

1. Elsa and Alan ran to their house because they saw: a) flames b) smoke c) a crowd
2. Outside their house Elsa and Alan found: a) their family b) Elsa's father c) some people
3. Elsa's father lived: a) with them b) in the next house c) in the front room
4. Alan went into the house because he wanted: a) to see the fire b) to talk to Elsa's father c) to save Elsa's father
5. When Alan found him, Elsa's father was: a) behind the door b) on the stairs c) in bed
6. Alan brought Elsa's father out of the house: a) in his arms b) in his coat c) on his back

C What do the words in italics refer to?

1. But *he* knew *she* was right.
2. *He* lived with *them*.
3. "*They*'ll be here any minute."

D Answer these questions with yes or no.

Did	Elsa go into the house?	1
	Alan go into the front room?	2
	Alan find Elsa's father easily?	3
	Elsa's father walk out of the house?	4
	the people in the crowd help Alan?	5
	Elsa's father go to hospital?	6
	Elsa's father intend to start the fire?	7

E Put these sentences in the correct order.

1. Elsa's father went to bed.
2. Smoke came out of the front room window.
3. Elsa's old father stayed at home.
4. Elsa's father did not know this.
5. Elsa and Alan went for a walk.
6. The neighbours phoned for the fire engine.
7. Elsa's father left his newspaper near the electric fire.
8. Elsa's father was asleep.
9. The newspaper began to burn.
10. Elsa's father was reading the newspaper in the front room.

F Guided composition. Use the sentences in E to complete this paragraph.

One evening, Elsa and Alan . . . . Elsa's old father, who lived with them, . . . , reading . . . . Later on, . . . , leaving . . . . Soon . . . . But Elsa's father . . . , because . . . . In a short time . . . , so . . . .

G Vocabulary practice. Complete these sentences, using the words in the box.

ambulance	back	fault	matter	smoke
asleep	crowd	fire	sign	upstairs

1 I'm sorry they disturbed you while you were . . . . It really wasn't my . . . .
2 Luckily my room is . . . , and at the . . . of the house too, so it's quite peaceful!
3 There's no . . . of any flames, but I'm sure I can smell . . . .
4 Please don't leave the electric . . . on when you go out.
5 What on earth's the . . . ? There's a big . . . in the street and an . . . is just coming!

H Discussion

Elsa's father started a fire in the house. What are other causes of fires in the house? Have you ever (nearly) caused a fire?

4

> **Read and decide.**
> 1) The woman wanted/did not want to cut the tree down.
> 2) In the end she was glad/sorry.

We had an enormous apple tree in our garden only a few yards from the kitchen window.

"We really must cut that tree down," my husband said, soon after we moved into the house. "I'm sure it's dangerous."

5 "Don't be silly," I said. I quite liked the tree myself. "It's quite safe. It isn't going to fall down on the house!"

"Well, I read something in the paper only the other day," he said. "A tree crashed into a woman's bedroom during a storm. She was going to get rid of the tree – and now she's in hospital!"

10 In the end, after several arguments of this kind, we asked a couple of workmen to come along and cut the tree down. It was not an easy job. In fact, it took them all morning. But at last the tree was lying on the ground.

"What about the roots?" the men asked. "Shall we take them out too or leave them?"

15 "Oh, take them out," I said. "Let's make a good job of it!"

This took all afternoon and I was beginning to think about the size of the bill! There was also a big hole in the garden!

"You'll be able to put all your old rubbish in there!" the men said as they left.

20 My husband climbed down into the hole and began to look around.

"Hey, look!" he called up to me. "There are some old coins here! And I think they're gold!"

I climbed down into the hole and we started to dig around, hoping to find some more coins. We did – and we also found a small metal box. We broke
25 it open. It was full of jewellery – rings, necklaces, and bracelets!

"Gosh!" I said, "I suppose someone hid these things in the ground – perhaps during a war!"

"They're probably worth a small fortune!" my husband said. "Well, aren't you glad now that you got rid of that old tree?"

A Find these words and phrases in the text:

enormous (*line 1*); in the end (*line 10*); make a good job of it (*line 15*); rubbish (*line 18*); coins (*line 21*); suppose (*line 26*); got rid of (*line 29*).

Now choose the right meaning.

1. removed
2. do it very well
3. very big
4. think
5. finally
6. things you do not want
7. money made of metal

B Choose the right answer.

1. The man wanted to get rid of the apple tree because it was:
   a) too near the house b) too old c) too big
2. The man's wife liked the tree but in the end she: a) went to hospital b) agreed c) helped to cut the tree down
3. The men who came to cut the tree down: a) had to work hard b) argued a lot c) worked during a storm
4. The workmen made a big hole because: a) they were looking for money b) they wanted to hide some rubbish c) they took out the roots of the tree
5. When the man climbed down into the hole, he found: a) some money b) some rubbish c) some apples
6. Later, the man and his wife found a box. The things in the box were: a) valuable b) important c) useful

C What do the words in italics refer to?

1. "*It*'s quite safe."
2. "... and now *she*'s in hospital."
3. "Shall we take *them* out too or leave them?"
4. "You'll be able to put all your old rubbish in *there*."
5. We *did*, and we also found a small metal box.
6. *It* was full of jewellery.
7. "*They*'re probably worth a fortune!"

D Put in the correct word.

1. ... wanted to cut the tree down.
2. ... was not worried about the tree.
3. ... had to work all day.
4. ... left a big hole in the garden.
5. ... found some coins in the hole.
6. ... found a box full of jewellery.

E Who said it?

1. "We really must cut that tree down."
2. "It's quite safe."
3. "What about the roots?"
4. "Let's make a good job of it!"
5. "They're probably worth a fortune!"

F Guided composition. Complete this extract from the man's diary.

Wednesday March 1st Two . . . came today to get rid of that . . . – the one that was just a few . . . from . . . . In the morning, they . . . the tree . . . . Then, in the . . . , they . . . out. As you can imagine, they left . . . in the . . . . However, that's not all! I climbed down into . . . and found . . . . Then we both found . . . . It was full of . . . ! Well, we're both glad we . . . that old tree!

G Vocabulary practice. Complete these sentences, using the words in the box.

coins	enormous	hole	rid of	workmen
dangerous	hid	jewellery	rubbish	worth

1 What shall we do with all this old . . . ? Oh, throw it in that . . . at the end of the garden.
2 The . . . made a very good job of the kitchen – but the bill was absolutely . . . !
3 She put all her . . . in a small metal box and then . . . it in her bedroom!
4 You say the car's safe – but I think it's . . . ! So let's get . . . it!
5 I've just found these old . . . in the garden. Do you think they're . . . anything?

H Discussion

Have you ever found anything valuable? (Where? What was it?)
People often find old things in the ground (or in the sea). Do you think they should keep them or give them to a museum?

5

Read and decide. This story is about: a) two policemen b) two thieves c) two friends

The two men, Lacey and Barnes, waited in their car about a quarter of a mile from the big house. They sat there in the darkness, smoking, hardly talking. It was now a little after midnight.

At last they saw a light in one of the upstairs windows. It flashed once, twice, three times. "That's the signal," Lacey said. Both men got out of the car. They were wearing dark clothes. They now put on gloves. Lacey had a small bag of tools.

"Can I bring the gun?" Barnes asked.

"How many times must I tell you! No guns!" Lacey snapped. "Not while you're working with me."

They entered the garden through a small side gate.

"I hope there aren't any dogs," Barnes said as they crept round the edge of the garden. They were going towards the back of the house.

"There are no dogs and no people here," Lacey told him. "Except for our friend upstairs. Now keep quiet and follow me!"

They entered a big yard at the back of the house.

"That's the window over there," Lacey said, pointing to a small window near the kitchen door. "You wait here. I'll get through the kitchen window. If I can't open the door, you'll have to climb through the window too."

Lacey crossed the yard. He opened the window without difficulty and climbed through. But the kitchen door was locked and the key was not there. He went to the window and whistled to Barnes.

"You'll have to climb through the window, too," he said.

Just at that moment they heard the sound of a car. It was approaching the house at great speed and its lights lit up the house as it got nearer. People got out and they could hear voices.

"It's the police!" Barnes said. "It's a trap. I knew it!"

"Don't panic!" Lacey told him. "Now listen to me. Go back to the car and wait for me there. I'll join you as soon as I can. Off you go – and keep well in the shadows."

A Find these words and phrases in the text:

hardly (*line 2*); flashed (*line 4*); edge (*line 12*); yard (*line 16*); at great speed (*line 25*); panic (*line 28*); keep well (*line 29*).

Now choose the right meaning.
1. be afraid
2. a piece of open ground
3. shone
4. not very much
5. stay as much as possible
6. side
7. very quickly

B Choose the right answer.
1. Lacey and Barnes were waiting for: a) midnight b) a signal c) a friend
2. The signal told them to: a) go to the house b) stop smoking c) stop talking
3. Barnes wanted to: a) put on his gloves b) take his tools c) take his gun
4. Lacey and Barnes went to the house: a) quietly b) quickly c) silently
5. Lacey got into the house. He then wanted to: a) open the door b) break down the door c) open the window
6. Before Barnes could get into the house: a) people shouted b) there was a fire c) a car came
7. Barnes was afraid that the police were trying to: a) catch them b) kill them c) hurt them
8. Lacey and Barnes went away from the house: a) one after the other b) together c) without lights

C What do the words in italics refer to?
1. *They* sat *there* in the darkness.
2. "There are no dogs and no people *here*," Lacey told *him*.
3. The key was not *there*.
4. Its lights lit up the house as *it* got nearer.
5. "Wait for me *there*."

D Which of these statements suggest that Lacey and Barnes were thieves?
1. They had a car.
2. They were wearing dark clothes.
3. They put on gloves.
4. Barnes wanted to take a gun.
5. They went through a small side gate.
6. Barnes was afraid of dogs.
7. Lacey climbed through a window.
8. Lacey could whistle.
9. They ran away when the car came.

E Put these sentences in the right order.

1 Lacey could not open the kitchen door.
2 Lacey and Barnes came to a yard.
3 A car approached the house.
4 Lacey and Barnes entered the garden through a small gate.
5 Lacey crossed the yard to the kitchen.
6 Lacey got into the house through a small window.
7 Lacey and Barnes crept round the side of the garden.
8 Lacey called to Barnes.
9 Lacey told Barnes to wait.

F Guided composition. Use the sentences in E to complete this paragraph.

Lacey and Barnes . . . . They . . . until . . . . Lacey . . . . Then he . . . and . . . . But he . . . , so he . . . . Just at that moment, however, ...

G Vocabulary practice. Complete these sentences, using the words in the box.

| except | gun | midnight | quiet | whistle |
| gloves | key | panic | signal | yard |

1 We arrived very late – after . . . , in fact. The door was locked and I hadn't got a . . . !
2 The bag was completely empty . . . for a pair of dark . . . .
3 When I give the . . . , run round the edge of the . . . three times! Right! Off you go!
4 Don't . . . ! He hasn't got a . . . and he isn't dangerous.
5 Please keep . . . ! It disturbs me when you . . . like that.

H Discussion

Do you like detective stories? Who is your favourite author?
What is your favourite book?
Suggest an ending for this story.

20

6

> **Read and decide.** Ann's diary is mainly about: a) food b) hostel life c) lectures

Sept 30 I moved into the hostel today — an ugly concrete building and near a busy main road too. My room is small but quite pleasant. I must get some posters for the walls, though. I met a few fellow students at supper (the food was awful!). They all look much younger than me. They *are*, of course!

Oct 7 Lectures began last Monday. So far they haven't been very interesting (except for the man who lectures on drama. He's first class). Personally, I'd much rather go to the library and read, but I have to attend ten lectures a week. Those are the 'rules'! Well, at least you meet people there.

Oct 12 I really don't like life in the hostel at all. The food is bad and the students are noisy. They stay up half the night and play games in the corridor outside my room. When on earth do they sleep? When do they work? And, on top of that, I don't like my room. It's just like living in a box! It looks even smaller now, with the posters on the wall!

Oct 26 I tried to explain some of my problems to my supervisor today. She listened — but that was about all. "You have to go to lectures, you know, Ann," she told me. "And the hostel *is* cheap and convenient." 'Cheap and convenient'! Well, it isn't 'cheap' if you can't eat the food and it isn't 'convenient' if you can't sleep at night!

Oct 30 I can't believe it! Three other students — I met them at a lecture and they're all about my own age — have invited me to share a flat with them. It's in an old house and it has its own kitchen, so we can cook for ourselves. And my room — right at the top of the house — is fantastic!

Nov 10 I moved into my new room last Sunday. I feel really happy. Life is going to be so much more fun from now on!

A Find these words and phrases in the text:

hostel (*line 1*); awful (*line 4*); lectures (*line 5*); so far (*line 5*); attend (*line 7*); share (*line 20*).

Now choose the right meaning.

1 go to
2 talks
3 have a part of
4 a place where students live
5 until now
6 very bad

B Choose the right answer.

1 Ann liked the hostel at first except for: a) her room b) the food c) the students

2 Ann went to lectures because: a) she was interested in drama b) she wanted to go c) she had to go
3 Ann complained about the students because: a) they disturbed her b) they did not work c) they did not sleep
4 Ann discussed her problems with her supervisor. Her supervisor did not: a) help her b) listen to her c) like her
5 Some students invited Ann to share a flat with them. Ann was: a) interested b) sorry c) excited
6 In the flat Ann will be able to: a) have her own kitchen b) cook in her room c) cook her own food

C Give the words or phrases for these pronouns.

1 *It* was near a busy main road.
2 Ann needed *some* for the walls of her room.
3 You could meet other students *there*.
4 The students made a lot of noise *there*.
5 *She* wasn't very interested in Ann's problems.
6 *It* was in an old house.
7 *It* was right at the top of the house.

D Make true sentences.

Ann	liked / didn't like	going to lectures.	1
		cooking her own food.	2
		living in the hostel.	3
		working in the library.	4
		eating hostel food.	5
		living in her new room.	6

E Answer these questions with yes or no.

Did Ann	get some posters for her room?	1
	go to lectures?	2
	want to play games in the corridor?	3
	agree with her supervisor?	4
	stay in the hostel?	5

F Guided composition. Complete this paragraph.

For the first few weeks, Ann lived in . . . . It was an . . ., not far from a . . ., but she quite liked it. Her room was . . ., but . . . . But then she began to dislike hostel life, mainly because the food was ... and the students were .... She began to dislike her room, too: it was just like ...! But then something fantastic happened: three other students, all of them about ..., invited her to ... with them. It was in ..., with its own ..., so that they could .... But, most of all, Ann liked ..., which was right ....

G Vocabulary practice. Complete these sentences, using the words in the box.

| attends | cheap | fantastic | library | rather |
| awful | convenient | first class | posters | share |

1 When he's busy, he hardly ever ... lectures. He stays in the ... all day and reads.
2 Thanks for those ... you gave me for my room. They're ...!
3 What's the hostel like? Well, personally, I think it's ..., except for the food. That's ...!
4 Which would you ... do – live alone or ... a house with other students?
5 I took the flat because it was .... But I'm afraid it's not very ... because it's so far from the main road.

H Discussion

Ann didn't like living in the hostel. Would you like to live in one? What are the advantages and disadvantages of living a) in a hostel; b) in a flat; c) at home?

23

7

> **Read and decide.** The old man told the traveller about: a) his present b) his past c) his future

A few years ago, while I was on holiday in the Himalayas, I stopped for the night in a small village. It was a very poor place and there was no proper hotel, but the owner of a restaurant offered me a bed for the night.

"Please wait here," he said, pointing to a table just outside his restaurant, "while I prepare your room."

It was a beautiful evening. The sun was setting behind the dark mountains and the stars were just beginning to come out. The villagers were lighting fires for their evening meals and there was a pleasant smell of wood smoke in the air.

Then I noticed that I was no longer alone. Someone was sitting at the table beside me. It was an old man with a long white beard. His clothes were dirty and almost in rags.

"What do you want?" I asked. "Let me tell your fortune, sir," he said. I laughed. "I don't believe in that sort of thing," I told him. All the same, the old man took hold of my hand. "I can tell you your future," he said. I tried to take my hand away, but the old man held on to it, gently but very firmly.

"Very well," I said. "But first of all tell me about my past. If you can tell me about that, I'll let you tell me about the future too." The old man looked hard at my hand for a long time without speaking. I smiled to myself. "He can't do it," I thought.

Then, in a low soft voice, the old man began to tell me about my childhood. He talked about my family and the town I used to live in. He went on to tell me about my life in different parts of the world.

Every word he said was true! "Stop!" I said. "How can you know all these things?" "I know about the past and the present," the old man replied. "And I also know about the future. Are you ready to hear about your future too?"

I hesitated. Did I really want to know?

Just at that moment, the owner of the restaurant came out. "Your room is ready now, sir," he said. "Oh! I thought I heard voices. Were you talking to someone?"

I looked round. The old man was not there. "Yes," I said. I described the old man. "Oh, him!" the owner of the restaurant said. "That's the village lunatic! He thinks he can tell people's fortunes! I hope he wasn't a nuisance!"

A Find these words and phrases in the text:

proper (*line 2*); almost in rags (*line 12*); all the same (*line 14*); very well (*line 17*); hard (*line 19*); hesitated (*line 27*).

24

Now choose the right meaning.
1. all right
2. in spite of this
3. waited
4. real
5. old and torn
6. very much

B Choose the right answer.
1. The traveller was looking for: a) somewhere to sleep b) something to eat c) something to do
2. The traveller sat outside because: a) he was waiting for his room b) it was a pleasant evening c) the restaurant was small
3. The old man wanted to talk about: a) the village b) money c) the traveller's future
4. The traveller asked to hear about his past life because: a) he did not believe in the old man b) he did not want to know about his future c) it was interesting
5. What the old man told the traveller was: a) funny b) correct c) different
6. The old man wanted to talk about the traveller's future. The traveller: a) was afraid b) could not speak c) could not decide
7. The owner of the restaurant thought that the old man was: a) clever b) mad c) unhappy

C Make true sentences.

The old man	lived in the village.	1
	was very poor.	2
	worked in the restaurant.	3
	asked for money.	4
	knew the traveller well.	5
	did not annoy the traveller.	6

D Copy this table and complete it with the phrases below.

Places	
Time of day	
People	
Events	

25

a traveller / an old man tells a traveller about his past / outside a restaurant / an old man / a village in the Himalayas / late evening / a restaurant owner

E   Put these sentences in the right order.

1   The old man told the traveller about his past.
2   A traveller was sitting at a table outside a restaurant.
3   The owner of the restaurant came out.
4   The traveller asked to hear about his past.
5   The traveller never heard about his future.
6   Again the old man offered to tell the traveller about his future.
7   An old man came and sat down beside the traveller.
8   The old man vanished.
9   The old man wanted to tell the traveller about his future.
10 The traveller hesitated.

F   Guided composition. Use the sentences in E to complete this paragraph.

One evening, while a traveller . 2 , an old man . 7 . The old man . 9 , but the traveller . . . first. So the old man . . . and then again . 6 . The traveller . 4 . . Just at that moment . 10 . The old man . . 8 , so the traveller . 5 . !

G   Vocabulary practice. Complete these sentences, using the words in the box.

| beard | fortune | hotel | nuisance | rags | world |
| childhood | gentle | lunatic | proper | voice | |

1   What did he look like? Well, he had a long . . . and his clothes were almost completely in . . . .
2   Let's look for a . . . restaurant. Perhaps there's one in that . . . over there.
3   Please don't be a . . . ! I don't want you to tell my . . . , thanks!
4   Does he really keep a gorilla in his garden? Well, in that case he must be a . . . !
5   Is it true you spent your . . . in different parts of the . . . ?
6   Everyone likes her . . . – probably because it's soft and . . . .

H   Discussion

Do you believe that people can know about the future? Why (not)? Has anyone ever told your future? What did they tell you?

8

> **Read and decide.** Roy had a problem. Did he find the answer to it?

Roy was always tired when he woke up in the morning.

"I really can't understand it," his brother said. "You go to bed earlier than I do and you get up later. I know you sleep well because you snore a lot! In fact, you sometimes keep me awake half the night! So why are you tired in the morning? It doesn't make sense!"

"Perhaps it's because I dream so much," Roy suggested.

"But dreaming is good for you," his brother told him. "All the doctors and psychiatrists agree about that."

"Maybe," Roy replied. "But the trouble is, I always dream about hard work! Last night, for example, I dreamt I was a miner. I went down the mine almost as soon as I fell asleep – and I dreamt that I was digging coal all night long. I was worn out in the morning! Then, a few nights ago, I dreamt I was a sailor. I was on one of those old fashioned sailing ships. We were crossing the Atlantic and there was a terrific storm. We had to struggle for hours to stop the ship from going down. It's always like that. In the past few weeks, I've dreamt I was a waiter, a lorry driver and a football player. I never have a nice easy job!"

"I was reading an article about sleep in a magazine the other day," his brother said. "The writer's advice was: try to relax before you go to sleep."

"But how?" Roy asked.

"Well, why don't you listen to some music? Something pleasant."

Roy was willing to try anything. But what sort of music? He liked pop music, but that was probably too noisy. So he decided to play some classical music and, just before he went to bed that night, he put on a record of Mozart. In fifteen minutes he was fast asleep.

"Well?" his brother asked him at breakfast next morning. "Did it work?"

Roy yawned. "Well," he said, "I didn't dream about hard work for once. I dreamt I was conducting an orchestra. The trouble was, the players weren't very good and we had to keep on playing the same piece again and again. In the end, we practised all night! I can tell you, I feel more tired this morning than I usually do!"

A Find these words and phrases in the text:

agree (*line 8*); worn out (*line 12*); struggle (*line 14*); willing to (*line 22*); fast (asleep) (*line 25*); for once (*line 27*).

Now choose the right meaning.
1 completely
2 very tired
3 on this occasion
4 have the same idea
5 work very hard
6 ready to

B Choose the right answer.

1 Roy had a problem. He: a) went to bed late b) was tired in the morning c) couldn't sleep
2 Roy's brother: a) kept him awake b) did not believe him c) could not understand this
3 In his dreams Roy: a) was always in trouble b) had to work hard c) travelled a lot
4 Roy's brother advised him to: a) listen to music b) sleep less c) read a magazine
5 Roy chose classical music because it was: a) quick b) easy c) quiet
6 Roy felt tired the next morning because: a) he didn't like the players b) he didn't like the music c) he had to work all night

C Give the words or phrases for these pronouns.

1 Roy dreamt that he worked down *one*.
2 Roy dreamt that he crossed the Atlantic on *one*.
3 Roy's brother read *one* in a magazine.
4 Roy played *one* before he went to sleep.
5 Roy dreamt that he conducted *one*.

D Match the statements in table 1 with the consequences in table 2.

1

Roy snored a lot.	1
Roy always dreamt about hard work.	2
There was a terrible storm.	3
Roy played some quiet music.	4
The players in the orchestra weren't very good.	5

2

He was tired in the morning.	a
He fell asleep quickly.	b
He kept his brother awake.	c
They had to practise all night.	d
The ship nearly went down.	e

E Guided composition. Complete this paragraph. It is from the magazine that Roy's brother read.

Many of our readers have problems because they cannot . . . , and therefore they . . . when they . . . in the morning. Some people think that this is because they . . . . However, this is not true. Doctors and psychiatrists . . . that . . . . Of course it is important to . . . before you . . . . For example, you can . . . . This will help you to go to sleep quickly and to sleep well.

F Vocabulary practice. Complete these sentences, using the words in the box.

advice	awake	magazine	pop	psychiatrist	relax
article	earlier	orchestra	practise	record	worn out

1 Can you give me some . . . ? I have to buy a . . . for my sister, and she doesn't like . . . music.
2 I feel . . . this morning. That storm kept me . . . half the night.
3 There's a very interesting . . . in this . . . about dreams. It's by a famous . . . .
4 "You work too hard!" my doctor told me. "Try to . . . in the evenings and go to bed . . . ."
5 What a terrible . . . ! The players really need to . . . more, don't they?

G Discussion

Do you dream a lot? What sort of dreams do you often have? What is the nicest (worst) dream you have ever had?

9

> **Read and decide.** Jane found something in the park. 1) What was it? 2) Where is it now?

Jane's great passion in life was animals. She had dozens of books about them. The walls of her bedroom were covered with pictures of animals, just as other girls of her age had posters of popstars.

She used to keep animals in the garden and, if she could, she brought them into the house too. Usually, however, her mother caught her.

"Get those animals out of here!" she used to shout. "If you must keep them, use the shed at the end of the garden!"

Most of Jane's animals were quite small: rabbits, mice, birds — that sort of thing. But one day something quite big came her way.

Jane's mother noticed that she was spending quite a lot of time in the shed. She also noticed that food was disappearing from the house — especially bread and fruit. One evening she decided to go down to the shed to see for herself.

As she stood outside the door of the shed, she could hear Jane talking to someone inside. "She's got a friend in there with her," she thought. She opened the door and looked in. At first she could only see Jane sitting on the ground. Then she made out the shape of an animal sitting beside Jane. Two huge eyes stared up at her. She nearly screamed. It was a gorilla!

"Jane! Where on earth...?" she started to say. But then she remembered. A few days before, a young gorilla escaped from the zoo and, in spite of every effort to find it, the animal simply vanished.

"I found it wandering through the park," Jane explained. "It seemed so lonely! I talked to it and we became friends at once. And then it followed me back here..."

"Well, you know you can't keep it," her mother said. "You'd better phone the police and explain."

Not long after, the police came and also a van from the zoo. Nobody was even angry with Jane when she told her story. The police knew all about Jane and her animals. And the zoo keeper said: "I can see that Gor likes you. But we need him back at the zoo! But you can come and see him as often as you like. We'll send you a free pass!"

These days Jane has almost given up collecting small animals — but you can often find her talking to her friend Gor at the zoo!

A Find these words in the text:

shed (*line 7*); disappearing (*line 11*); shape (*line 16*); screamed (*line 17*); simply (*line 20*); lonely (*line 22*).

Now choose the right meaning.

1. just
2. gave a loud cry
3. hut
4. unhappy because it was alone
5. form
6. going

B Choose the right answer.

1. Jane was very interested in: a) animals b) music c) pictures
2. Jane sometimes tried to take animals into the house. Her mother: a) did not like this b) put them in the shed c) did not know
3. Jane's mother went to the shed because she wanted to find: a) the animals b) the food c) Jane's friends
4. Before Jane's mother went into the shed, she: a) looked through the window b) talked to herself c) listened at the door
5. When Jane's mother first saw the gorilla, she was: a) afraid b) pleased c) surprised
6. The gorilla belonged to: a) a park b) a zoo c) the police
7. The gorilla followed Jane home because it wanted to: a) be with her b) leave the park c) talk to her
8. Jane told the police her story. She said: a) "The gorilla is a friend of mine." b) "The gorilla belongs to me." c) "I found the gorilla in the park."

C Give the words or phrases for these pronouns.

1. Jane had pictures of animals *there*.
2. Jane kept animals *there*.
3. Jane found the gorilla *there*.
4. The police went *there*.
5. Jane often goes *there* these days.

D Right or wrong?

1. Jane kept animals in her bedroom.
2. Jane took a lot of fruit from the house.
3. Jane wasn't afraid of the gorilla.

E Match the statements in table 1 with the reasons in table 2.

1.

Jane took food from the house.	1
Jane began to spend a lot of time in the shed.	2
Jane's mother used to shout at her.	3
The gorilla vanished.	4
Jane phoned the police.	5

2	It was in Jane's shed.	a
	She tried to bring animals into the house.	b
	She needed it for the gorilla.	c
	She had to tell them about the gorilla.	d
	She had a gorilla there.	e

F Guided composition. Complete this conversation between Jane and the police sergeant.

J: Hello? This is Jane Hunt.
PS: Hello, Jane. What can I do for you?
J: Well, you remember that . . . that escaped . . . ?
PS: Of course. Why, have you found it?
J: . . . .
PS: Good! Where is it now?
J: . . . .
PS: All right. Keep it there and I'll phone the . . . . We'll come and get it in a . . . . But where on earth did you find it?
J: Well, I was walking through the . . . and I saw . . . there. It was very . . . . I talked to it and we became . . . and it followed me . . . .

G Vocabulary practice. Complete these sentences, using the words in the box.

apples	fruit	hesitate	screamed	shed	vanished
collect	given up	lonely	shape	spite	

1 She has lots of friends, but in . . . of that, she's very . . . .
2 If you want anything, just ask for it. Please don't . . . !
3 A friend of mine kept some rabbits in the . . . at the end of his garden. Then one day they escaped and simply . . . !
4 I used to . . . posters of popstars, but I've . . . that . . . now.
5 I'm very fond of . . . , especially . . . .
6 Then, through the window, I saw the . . . of a huge animal. I nearly . . . !

H Discussion

Jane was very fond of animals. Are you? Do you have any pets? (Would you like to keep a pet?) What sort of problems can pets cause? Would you like to work in a zoo? Why (not)?

10

> **Read and decide.**
> 1) The balloon landed safely / crashed.
> 2) The balloon came down on some mountains / near a farm.

The balloon took off quite slowly but, within minutes, they were high above the field. The spectators were still waving to them but soon they too were out of sight.

It was Andy's first trip in a balloon and he felt nervous. Pete, his companion, knew all about balloons – he went up in one every weekend if the weather was fine – but he was too busy to answer Andy's questions.

"Just enjoy it," he said as they took off. "It's a wonderful experience." Andy was not sure. But the view was interesting. He passed the time trying to make out landmarks – villages, farms and rivers. Everything looked so different from the air!

"Where are we heading for?" he asked Pete. Pete pointed towards the north.

"That's our general direction for the moment," he said. "Unfortunately this wind keeps pushing us towards those hills." He pointed to some mountains in the west. "There's nothing to worry about, though. I'll take the balloon higher."

A quarter of an hour later Pete was beginning to look worried. They were close to some very thick clouds. "I don't like the look of these," he said. A few minutes later they were in the middle of the clouds and they could see nothing. Suddenly it was very cold.

"I wasn't expecting weather like this," Pete said. "Well, let's have some coffee to warm us up." He poured out two cups and handed one to Andy. Andy needed a hot drink at that moment.

"We're still going towards those mountains, aren't we?" he asked Pete.

"Yes, but don't worry," Pete replied. "We'll go right over the top."

They drifted on and on through the clouds. Every moment Andy expected the balloon to hit the side of the mountain. But it never happened. Suddenly they were out in the sunlight again.

"The trouble is," Pete said, "I'm not sure exactly where we are now!"

Andy looked down. "Isn't that a farm down there?" he asked, pointing to some buildings. "Why don't we land and ask?"

Pete hesitated. They were lost, but he did not want to ask for help.

"All right," he said in the end.

A few minutes later, they made a perfect landing only a couple of hundred yards from the farmhouse. The farmer came out to greet them.

"You're a long way from home!" he said in answer to Pete's question. "Well, we'll think about that later. Come in and join us for tea. It isn't often that people come to visit us by balloon!"

A Find these words and phrases in the text:

took off (*line 1*); spectators (*line 2*); nervous (*line 4*); heading for (*line 11*); close to (*line 18*); drifted (*line 26*); perfect (*line 34*).

Now choose the right meaning:
1 very good
2 afraid
3 near
4 moved slowly and without direction
5 left the ground
6 going towards
7 people who were watching

B Choose the right answer.

1 As they took off, Andy wanted to: a) see the spectators b) land in the field c) talk to his friend
2 Andy tried to identify places on the ground but this was not: a) easy b) possible c) interesting
3 Pete wanted to go to the north. Instead the wind took them to: a) the south b) the west c) the east
4 Pete began to worry when they were near some: a) mountains b) winds c) clouds
5 Andy tried to identify places on the ground but this was not: c) cold
6 While they were going through the clouds, Andy felt: a) nervous b) excited c) bored
7 When Andy saw the farm, he wanted to: a) ask for help b) look at the building c) stop for tea
8 Pete asked the farmer: a) "Have you ever seen a balloon before?" b) "Who are you?" c) "Where are we?"
9 The farmer: a) sent them home b) wanted to look at their balloon c) invited them to his house

C Make true sentences.

Andy Pete	often went up in balloons.	1
	knew nothing about balloons.	2
	felt nervous as the balloon went up.	3
	wanted to go towards the north.	4
	brought some coffee with him.	5
	lost his way.	6
	saw the farm first.	7
	did not want to land.	8

D Put these sentences in the right order.

1 A wind pushed the balloon towards some mountains in the west.
2 A farmer invited Andy and Pete to tea.
3 Andy and Pete drank some coffee.
4 The balloon went up into the air.
5 Andy saw a farm.
6 Andy and Pete got into some clouds.
7 Andy and Pete landed.
8 Andy tried to make out landmarks.
9 Andy and Pete came out into the sunlight.
10 People waved to Andy and Pete.
11 The balloon went over the top of the mountains.
12 The balloon went towards the north.

E Guided composition. Use the sentences in D to complete this paragraph.

As the balloon . . . , people . . . . Andy passed the time . . . .
The balloon . . . , but a wind began . . . and soon . . . . As they
drifted through the clouds, they . . . . Luckily, . . . and
suddenly . . . . Looking down, Andy . . . . They . . . and the
farmer there . . . .

F Vocabulary practice. Complete these sentences, using the words in the box.

| balloon | field | nervous | out of sight | wave |
| clouds | head for | north | perfect | weather |

1 On a fine day, when the . . . is really good and there are no . . . , you can see the mountains from here.
2 I had a trip in a . . . last week. I didn't enjoy the experience, though. I felt . . . all the time.
3 Let's . . . that farm over there – to the . . . of the village.
4 The plane made a . . . landing in a small . . . beside a river.
5 Quick! . . . to those people before they are . . . .

G Discussion

Andy felt nervous when he went up in the balloon. Do you think
that you would be nervous too? What are some of the dangers
when you do this sort of thing?

11

> **Read and decide.** 1) Were the people on the motor boat pleased or annoyed with Robert? 2) Why?

It was a cold winter's afternoon. Robert paused for a moment as he crossed the bridge and looked down at the river below. There were hardly any boats on the river. Near the bridge, however, almost directly below, there was one small one, a canoe, with a boy in it. He was not even wearing many clothes,
5 Robert noticed. He shivered and walked on.

Just then he heard a cry. "Help! Help!" The cry definitely came from the river. Robert looked down. The boy was in the water and his canoe was floating away. "Help! Help!" he called again.

Robert was a good swimmer and he hesitated for only a moment. Taking
10 off his coat, he dived into the river. The icy water almost took his breath away, but in a matter of seconds he reached the boy. "Don't panic!" he said as he caught hold of him. "Just relax – and I'll soon get you out of the water."

But the boy began to struggle and shout something at him. Robert could not make out his words. "Don't panic," he said again and started to swim
15 towards the bank, dragging the boy with him. But at that moment he noticed a large motor boat under the bridge. There were several people on board, all looking in his direction. Robert decided to swim towards the boat.

"Give me a hand," he shouted as he got near the boat. He looked up into a row of faces. "It's funny," he thought. "They look angry." Silently the people
20 on the boat helped the boy aboard and wrapped him in a blanket. But they made no move to help Robert.

"Aren't you going to pull me out too?" Robert asked.

"You!" said one of the men. Robert noticed that he was standing next to a large camera. "You! Why, we were making a film and you spoilt a whole
25 afternoon's work! You can stay in the water!"

A Find these words and phrases in the text:

definitely (*line 6*); floating (*line 8*); dragging (*line 15*); wrapped (*line 20*); made no move (*line 21*); spoilt (*line 24*).

Now choose the right meaning.

1 did not try
2 pulling
3 ruined
4 certainly
5 moving on the water
6 covered

B Choose the right answer.

1 When Robert heard the cry for help, he was: a) still on the bridge b) looking at the river c) taking off his jacket

2. Robert dived into the river: a) to have a swim b) to get his coat c) to save the boy
3. The people on the boat: a) laughed at Robert b) did not speak to Robert c) left Robert in the water
4. The people on the boat wanted to make a film of the boy: a) with Robert b) in the water c) in his canoe

C Give the words or phrases for these pronouns.

1. *It* was almost directly below the bridge.
2. Robert took *it* off.
3. Robert started to swim towards *it*.
4. *It* was under the bridge.
5. The people on the boat wrapped the boy in *it*.
6. One of the men on the boat was standing next to *it*.

D Answer these questions.

1. What was the weather like?
2. Were there a lot of boats on the river?
3. Who was in the canoe?
4. Did Robert dive into the water quickly?
5. What did the boy do?
6. Could the people on the boat see Robert?
7. Did the people on the boat help the boy out of the water?
8. Did the people on the boat help Robert out of the water?
9. What were the people on the boat doing?

E Copy this table. Then complete it with the items below.

Time of	day	
	year	
Places	
People	
Events	

a motor boat / film people / winter / Robert / a boy / a bridge / afternoon / Robert 'saved' a boy / a river / He spoilt a film

F Guided composition. Complete this paragraph.

One cold . . . , some people were making . . . on a river. During the film, . . . had to fall out of his . . . into . . . , crying " . . . ". While they were filming this from their . . . under . . . , a man . . . off the bridge and tried to . . . the boy. He even brought . . . to their . . . under the bridge! As you can imagine, they were not exactly . . . about all this because it spoilt . . . .

G Vocabulary practice. Complete these sentences, using the words in the box.

| bank | camera | definitely | film | hand |
| board | crossed | dived | float away | spoil |

1 What are they doing on . . . that motor boat. Well, they've got an enormous camera, so perhaps they're making a . . . .
2 Give me a . . . , please. I think the canoe is starting to . . . .
3 We . . . the river in a matter of minutes and then sat down on the other . . . .
4 That man was . . . lucky! When he fell in the river, someone . . . into the icy water to save him!
5 Be careful! If you get that . . . wet, you'll . . . it.

H Discussion

Are you a good swimmer? Have you ever helped anyone like this? (Has anyone ever helped *you*?)
Suggest an ending for this story.

12

> **Read and decide.** 1) Which part of his car did Alex (= the writer) lose? 2) Where did he lose it?

I always enjoy the drive into Marley. It is a good straight road, with some pleasant views of the countryside on either side. There are woods and hills, villages and farms and, about halfway, a large lake. And because there is rarely much traffic on the road, I can usually enjoy the view as I drive along.

5 I was rather annoyed the other morning, therefore, when a small green car began to drive very close behind me. I went a little faster, hoping to leave the car behind. But whenever I slowed down, the little car caught up with me. The driver, a middle-aged man, was grinning and waving to me. However, I did not recognise either him or the car.

10 Again I began to drive a little faster but the little car caught up with me whenever I slowed down. "Perhaps I am doing something wrong," I thought. I checked my lights and my indicator, but they were both in order. And I certainly had not got a puncture. The man was a lunatic, I decided. Feeling rather cross, I drove off very fast, leaving the small green car behind. I did not slow
15 down until I got to Marley.

There are some traffic lights just before you cross the railway bridge into Marley and, as it happened, the lights turned red as I approached. I was still waiting there when the little green car caught up with me.

The driver got out and tapped on my window. I opened it. "Can I help you?"
20 I asked rather coldly. "I'm trying to help *you*!" the man said. "You see, your number plate fell off about fifteen miles back. I tried to attract your attention, but you didn't take any notice!"

A Find these words and phrases in the text:

straight (*line 1*); grinning (*line 8*); checked (*line 12*); in order (*line 12*); cross (*line 14*); attract (*line 21*).

Now choose the right meaning.

1 angry
2 tested
3 without bends
4 smiling
5 catch
6 working well

B Choose the right answer.

1 The driver of the small green car annoyed Alex because he wanted to: a) enjoy the view b) drive slowly c) stop halfway
2 Alex got away from the small green car by: a) driving very fast b) checking his lights c) waving to him

3 Alex stopped at the bridge because of: a) a train b) the traffic
  c) the traffic lights
4 The driver of the small green car wanted to: a) talk to Alex
  b) help Alex c) annoy Alex

C Give the words or phrases for these pronouns.

1 *He* usually usually enjoyed *them* as he drove there.
2 *He* drove very fast because he wanted to leave *it* behind.
3 *He* checked *them* in case something was wrong.
4 *He* stopped *there* because *they* were red.
5 *He* tapped on *it* because he wanted to speak to *him*.

D Answer these questions.

1 What was the road to Marley like?
2 Why did Alex usually drive slowly?
3 Who was in the small green car?
4 What did the driver of the small green car do?
5 Did Alex know the driver of the small green car?
6 What did Alex do before he drove off very fast?
7 Did Alex stop before he got to Marley?
8 Why did Alex stop at the railway bridge?
9 What did the driver of the small green car tell Alex?
10 Was Alex pleased (do you think)?

E Match the statements in table 1 with the reasons in table 2.

1

Alex	couldn't enjoy the view.	1
	checked his lights and indicator.	2
	drove fast.	3
	had to stop at the bridge.	4
	lost his number plate.	5

2

The traffic lights were red.	a
He wanted to get away from the green car.	b
The little green car was close behind him.	c
He didn't pay any attention to the driver of the green car.	d
He thought that something was wrong.	e

F Guided composition. Complete this paragraph.

The other day, as I was driving into Marley, the number plate of the car in front of me fell off. The car . . . quite slowly at the time (the driver . . . probably . . . the view!), so I . . . him and . . . . But instead of stopping, the man began to . . . a little faster. This happened several times until, in the end, the man . . . very fast, . . . me behind. Anyway, I . . . him at the traffic lights near the bridge into Marley. I . . . my car and . . . on his window. "Your number plate . . . about fifteen miles back," I told him. He looked really cross then!

G Vocabulary practice. Complete these sentences, using the words in the box.

attention	check	in order	slow down	traffic lights
caught up with	cross	puncture	traffic	view

1 I think the car in front has got a . . . . Try to attract the driver's . . . .
2 You'd better . . . . There are some . . . just ahead.
3 We'd better . . . the car before we leave, just to see that everything is . . . .
4 She went off without saying a word. I followed her, and when I . . . her, she looked very . . . .
5 There isn't much . . . on the road today. That's good, because it means we can enjoy the . . . as we drive along.

H Discussion

Can you drive? Do you like driving? Have you ever had any problems while you were driving?

13

Read and decide. What did Johnny want to be when he grew up? a) a teacher b) a policeman c) an explorer

Johnny was three when he ran away from home for the first time. Somebody left the garden gate open. Johnny wandered out, crossed some fields, and two hours later, arrived in the next village. He was just able to give his name and address.

By the time he was seven, Johnny used to vanish from home two to three times a year. Sometimes he covered quite long distances on foot. On other occasions he got on a bus or even a train, and simply sat there until someone asked for his ticket. Generally the police brought him home. "Why do you do it?" they used to ask. "You aren't unhappy at home, are you?" "Of course not," Johnny replied. "Then why?" "I just like seeing places," Johnny told them.

Johnny continued to 'see places' although everyone tried to stop him. His parents used to watch him closely, and so did his teachers; but sooner or later Johnny managed to slip away. As he grew older, his favourite trick was to hide on a long distance lorry. Sometimes he used to travel hundreds of miles before anyone discovered him.

It is hardly surprising that eventually Johnny managed to get on board a plane. He was twelve at the time. It was a cargo plane and, a few hours later, Johnny found himself in Cairo. How did he get on board? No one knows! According to Johnny himself, it was easy: he just went into the airport, walked along some corridors and got on board the nearest plane.

In spite of all this, Johnny did well at school. He enjoyed maths and languages and, perhaps not surprisingly, he was especially good at geography. "What do you want to be when you grow up?" his teachers asked him. Johnny did not take long to answer that question. "An explorer!" he answered. "But it's difficult to become an explorer in this modern age," they tried to tell him, "unless you go into space!" But it was no use: Johnny knew what he wanted!

Just before he left school, Johnny saw a notice in one of the daily papers. An expedition was about to go to Brazil to travel up the Amazon. There were vacancies for three young people 'willing to work hard and with a sense of adventure.' Johnny applied... and, two months later, he was on his way to Brazil.

A Find these words and phrases in the text:

covered (*line 6*); closely (*line 12*); slip away (*line 13*); cargo plane (*line 17*); notice (*line 27*); vacancies (*line 29*).

Now choose the right meaning.
1. plane carrying things
2. get away secretly
3. places
4. advertisement
5. walked
6. carefully

B Choose the right answer.

1. Johnny ran away from home because: a) he was young b) he was unhappy c) he liked travelling
2. As he grew older, Johnny began to: a) stay at home b) travel further c) hide from his parents
3. Johnny went to Cairo because: a) he liked geography b) a plane was going there c) he liked flying
4. Johnny wanted to become an explorer, but his teachers said: a) "You're too young." b) "Go to the moon instead." c) "It isn't easy these days."
5. In the end, Johnny: a) joined an expedition b) ran away from school c) worked for a newspaper

C Right or wrong?

1. Johnny could not talk when he ran away from home for the first time.
2. Johnny was happy at home.
3. The lorry drivers knew that Johnny was on their lorries.
4. Johnny was a good student.
5. Johnny read about the expedition to Brazil in a newspaper.

D Copy this table. Then complete it with the items below.

At the age of three		
By the age of seven		
As he grew older	Johnny	
At the age of twelve		
When he left school		

liked to travel on long distance lorries / joined an expedition to Brazil / ran away from home for the first time / went to Cairo by plane / vanished two or three times a year

E Guided composition. Use the information from the table in D and also information from the text to complete this paragraph.

Johnny became 'an explorer' very early in life. He first . . . at the age of three and on that occasion went as far as . . . . By the time he was seven, he used to . . . , sometimes travelling . . . ; on other occasions . . . or . . . . As he grew older, he . . . , sometimes going for . . . before anyone discovered him. Finally, at the age of twelve, he . . . ! It is not surprising, therefore, that when he . . . , Johnny . . . .

F Vocabulary practice. Complete these sentences, using the words in the box.

| adventure | cargo | hides | travels | unless |
| apply | geography | tickets | tricks | vacancies |

1 I see there are several . . . for jobs at the airport. Why don't you . . . for one?
2 She's very good at . . . , but that's hardly surprising, since she . . . so much!
3 I came back from Australia on a . . . boat. It was quite an . . . !
4 Sometimes he . . . from people all day. It's one of his favourite . . . .
5 . . . you put up a big notice, no one will know about the play and we'll never sell any . . . !

G Discussion

Johnny ran away from home. Have you ever run away from home? Have you ever wanted to? Why? Would you like to go on an expedition like Johnny? Where to?

14

> **Read and decide.** Mrs Green wanted to go to India. She asked the travel agent for: a) a hotel b) a ticket c) a guidebook

"A holiday abroad? Yes, of course, Mrs Green. I'm sure we can arrange something for you."

The travel agent smiled at the old lady across the counter. He knew her well. At one time, years before, she and her husband used to go to Brighton
5 every summer. In those days, he booked a family hotel for them. Then they started to take their holidays in France – and he got them their boat tickets. Later, when their children grew up, they 'discovered' Italy and Spain. He bought their air tickets or found cheap holidays for them.

But then, the previous autumn, Mr Green died. "Well, no more holidays
10 abroad for Mrs Green," he thought. "She'll probably start going to Brighton again!"

But he was wrong! Here she was, only a few months after her husband's death, back in his office asking about holidays abroad.

"Have you any particular place in mind?" he asked. "How about Portugal,
15 for instance? A nice, friendly place, with good weather..."

Mrs Green shook her head. "As a matter of fact," she said, "I was thinking of India!"

India! For a moment the travel agent was surprised, but then he thought: "Of course! Lots of people want to go to India these days. It's all these
20 programmes and films on TV. However, at *her* age..." "India...," he said. "Well, yes. I'm sure we can fix up something for you." He showed Mrs Green a brochure. "How about a two week tour, for example? Complete with air ticket, hotels, meals and guides. You'll see the really important places – and you won't have to think about a thing!"

25 "Thank you," said Mrs Green. "That's exactly what I *don't* want." The travel agent looked puzzled. "Look," Mrs Green went on. "I've got a guidebook of India here." She waved it at him. "It says you can go everywhere by bus or train. There are plenty of cheap hotels – and food is cheap too. So all I need is a cheap air ticket! Can you get me one or not?"

A Find these words in the text:

abroad (*line 1*); counter (*line 3*); booked (*line 5*); cheap (*line 8*); particular (*line 14*); brochure (*line 22*); tour (*line 22*).

Now choose the right meaning.

1 a kind of table in a shop
2 special
3 a journey to a number of places
4 in a foreign country
5 not costing much money
6 arranged
7 a small book giving information

B Choose the right answer.

1 The travel agent knew Mrs Green and her husband well because for many years he: a) helped them with their holidays b) went with them on holiday c) chose their holidays for them
2 When her husband died, the travel agent expected Mrs Green to: a) stop having holidays b) ask for cheap holidays c) have her holidays in England
3 At the time many people were interested in holidays in India because of: a) good weather b) TV programmes and films c) cheap hotels
4 Mrs Green wanted to: a) arrange her own holiday b) think about India c) read about India

C What do the words in italics refer to?

1 *He* knew *her* well.
2 *In those days* he booked a family hotel for *them*.
3 *She* waved *it* at *him*.

D Make true sentences.

The travel agent	suggested didn't suggest	a holiday in Brighton.	1
		a holiday in Portugal.	2
		a cheap holiday in India.	3
		a complete tour of India.	4
		a two week tour of India.	5

Mrs Green said she	wanted didn't want	to go to Portugal.	1
		to go abroad.	2
		to go to India.	3
		to go on a two week tour of India.	4
		to have a cheap air ticket.	5

E Guided composition. Complete this extract from Mrs Green's diary.

I went to the travel agent's today to try to . . . . I've used him for years. At one time, when the children . . . , he used to book . . . for us every year. Then, when the children . . . and we started to . . . , he used to get . . . for us. And when the children . . . , he used to find us . . . . Anyway, he was surprised today when I told him that I wanted . . . . First of all, he suggested . . . . I told him I . . . . He then suggested . . . . I told him I didn't want that. All I wanted was . . . ! Well, I hope he can get me one!

F Vocabulary practice. Complete these sentences, using the words in the box.

book	fix up	hotel	puzzled	travel agent
cheap	guidebook	previous	shakes	tour

1 There are plenty of . . . holidays abroad. Let's ask the . . . for some brochures.
2 If you . . . the hotel, I'll . . . everything else.
3 They arranged everything on the . . . . I didn't even need a . . . !
4 I'm really . . . . If you ask her a question, she just . . . her head!
5 They're staying in the same . . . again this year. I'm surprised, because on the . . . occasion, they grumbled about it all the time.

G Discussion

Mrs Green wanted a holiday that was 'different'. What would you do if you wanted a different kind of holiday? Where would you go to? Would you go alone? What was the best holiday you ever had?

15

> **Read and decide.** Rose (= the writer of this diary) has lost her job. 1) Does she want another one? 2) Does she get one?

Friday For once I have something important to put in my diary. Normally I have to *think* of something to write about – but today was different. Something special happened: I lost my job! Well, I'm going to bed now. I'll think about it in the morning.

Monday I woke up at 6.30. The sun was shining; the birds were singing (etc). For a while I felt really happy. Then I remembered: I hadn't got a job. I could stay in bed all morning – but I didn't want to. I went into the kitchen and made myself some tea. I sat drinking it by the window. People were hurrying to work. Some of them didn't look very happy. Perhaps they didn't want to work! "Fools!" I wanted to shout at them. "You fools! At least you have jobs!"

Later I went along to the Job Centre. I filled in a form and had an interview with a clerk. She was quite pleasant, really, but she asked me a lot of silly questions! Anyway, she hadn't got a job to offer me. I have to go back there on Wednesday.

Tuesday I called in at the bank today and checked my account. At least I'm not short of money – for the moment. Then I walked past the office where I used to work. Through the windows I could see people working inside. I felt envious! Afterwards, I sat in a cafe, thinking. If there's nothing at the Job Centre tomorrow, I'll ring my old friend Liz. She usually has some ideas.

Wednesday I saw a different clerk at the Job Centre today. He was not very encouraging. "You need to get some training," he said. "In computers, for example." In short, they haven't got a job for me! I'm definitely going to ring Liz in the morning.

Friday I rang Liz twice yesterday, but I couldn't get an answer. I felt very depressed. Then I went for a long walk and I felt much better. I came home and watched a TV programme – about unemployment! That depressed me again!

Saturday I finally managed to get through to Liz this morning. Actually, she was *pleased* when she heard I was looking for a job! "Good!" she said. "Just come and see me tomorrow, Rose, and I'll tell you all about my plans!" Then she rang off. So I'm going to see her tomorrow. But what *are* her plans, I wonder?

A Find these words and phrases in the text:

filled in (*line 11*); called in at (*line 15*); (am) not short of (*line 16*); depressed (*line 25*); get through to (*line 28*); rang off (*line 31*).

48

Now choose the right answer.
1 went to
2 completed
3 put the phone down
4 have enough
5 unhappy
6 speak to

B Choose the right answer.
1 On Monday morning Rose did not have to go to work. She felt:
  a) pleased b) sad c) tired
2 When she went to the Job Centre the first time, Rose: a) talked to a clerk b) nearly got a job c) wrote some letters
3 On her second visit to the Job Centre, the clerk told Rose:
  a) to prepare for a new job b) to get a computer c) to go back to her old office
4 Rose is probably going to get a job: a) at a Job Centre b) on TV c) with a friend

C Give the words or phrases for these pronouns.
1 Some of *them* didn't look very happy as they went *there*.
2 *She* asked Rose a lot of silly questions *there*.
3 Rose saw people working *there*.
4 Rose sat *there*, thinking.

D Ask and answer questions like this.
When did Rose lose her job? On Friday.
1 walk past her office
2 go for a long walk
3 first go to the Job Centre
4 go to see Liz
5 speak to Liz
6 visit her bank
7 go back to the Job Centre
8 try to speak to Liz
9 watch people going to work
10 watch a TV programme about unemployment

E Match these statements with the reasons in table 2.

1

Rose	had something important to write in her diary.	1
	went to the Job Centre.	2
	went to her bank.	3
	went for a long walk.	4
	wanted to speak to Liz.	5

2

She	was looking for a job.	a
	felt depressed.	b
	wanted her advice.	c
	lost her job.	d
	wanted to check her account.	e

F Guided composition. Complete this conversation between Rose and Liz.

R: Hello, Liz. It's me – Rose.
L: Hi! How are you?
R: Well, ...
L: Depressed? Why?
R: . . . .
L: Oh! When did that happen?
R: . . . .
L: Have you tried to get another one?
R: . . . . I've . . . twice this week already.
L: Hm, are you short of money?
R: . . . .
L: Now listen! This is really good news.
R: . . . ?
L: Come and see me tomorrow and I'll tell you all about it!

G Vocabulary practice. Complete these sentences, using the words in the box.

called in	clerks	envious	short of
check	depressed	get through	training

1 I feel very . . . ! I'd like to get some . . . in computers too!
2 Why are you looking so . . . ? You aren't . . . money again, are you?
3 One of the . . . from your office rang up. He wants you to go and . . . some accounts.
4 I couldn't . . . to her on the phone, so in the end I . . . at her office.

H Discussion

Liz probably had some plans to start her own business. What would you like to do if you could start *your* own business?

16

> **Read and decide.** 1) Who are the people in this story? 2) Are they all friends?

It was Saturday morning. Nicky and I were just finishing our shopping. "Let me see...," Nicky said. "We've been to the supermarket, the baker's and the greengrocer's... Is that the lot?"

I looked at my list. "I just need a couple of things from the chemist's," I told her. "All right," Nicky said. "While you're doing that, I'll just call in at the bookshop."

We arranged to meet at a cafe in a quarter of an hour. I arrived first. When Nicky came in, she looked quite excited.

"Did you find your book, then?" I asked as she sat down.

"Yes," Nicky said.

"Something special?" I asked. I was curious because Nicky was not a great reader, except for newspapers and magazines. She sometimes borrowed books, but she rarely bought them.

"Well, yes," Nicky admitted.

"What's all the mystery?" I asked. "Tell me all about it!"

"It isn't exactly a mystery, Kay," Nicky began. I waited for her to go on. "Well, do you remember that woman who used to live opposite the church – Miss Hunter?"

"The one who used to wear funny clothes and had a large dog? Wasn't she an artist?"

"Well, yes," Nicky said. "She *did* paint – but only as a hobby. As a matter of fact, she was a writer – and I've just bought her latest book!" Nicky took the book out of her bag and passed it across the table. The title was 'Death Comes to the Village'.

"A detective story," I said. "Hey, do you think we're in it?"

"I'm pretty sure *I* am," Nicky said, looking rather pleased with herself. "You see, Miss Hunter and I were quite good friends and she often said she was going to put me into her next book!"

"Shall we have a look?" I asked. But Nicky picked the book up and put it in her bag. "I'd like to read it first," she said. "But I'll lend it to you, of course..."

Some time passed after our meeting in the cafe and I heard nothing from Nicky. I decided to ring her up and ask about the book. "Oh, that!" she muttered.

"You don't sound very pleased," I said. "Weren't you in the book after all?"

"Yes," Nicky said. "I'm in the book all right! But who do you think I am? I'm the village postwoman! I pass on all the gossip in the village! I even open letters sometimes! I'm the most unpleasant person in the whole book! That woman is no friend of mine, I can tell you!"

A Find these words and phrases in the text:

the lot (*line 3*); curious (*line 11*); funny (*line 19*); hobby (*line 21*); latest (*line 22*); pretty (*line 26*); gossip (*line 37*).

Now choose the right answer.

1 everything
2 bad talk about people
3 strange
4 quite
5 most recent
6 interested
7 something you do in your spare time

B Choose the right answer.

1 While Kay was at the chemist's, Nicky: a) bought a book b) telephoned the bookshop c) went to the cafe
2 Miss Hunter wrote books but she also: a) made clothes b) was a detective c) painted pictures
3 Nicky bought the book because: a) she expected to be in it b) she liked Miss Hunter c) she liked detective stories
4 When Nicky read the book, she felt: a) angry b) depressed c) bored

C Make questions and answers.

Where / What	did	Nicky and Kay meet? / Nicky usually read? / Kay go before she went to the cafe? / Nicky and Kay do in the cafe?

She / They	went to the chemist's. / talked about the book. / met at the cafe. / read newspapers and magazines.

D Answer these questions.

1 Did Nicky and Kay go to the supermarket together?
2 Did Kay go to the chemist's alone?
3 Was Kay interested in Nicky's book?
4 Did Miss Hunter still live in the village?
5 Was this Miss Hunter's first book?
6 Did Nicky read the book?
7 Did Nicky tell Kay about the book?
8 Was Nicky really a postwoman?

E Write notes about Nicky's book.

Title of book
Type of book
Author
Personal details about author
Nicky's part in the book

F Guided composition. Complete this letter from Kay to a friend.

Have you heard about poor Nicky? She was a friend of . . . who lived . . . . Her name was . . . . (She had . . . and wore . . .). I thought she was . . . , but this was just . . . . She was really . . . . Anyway, she and Nicky became quite . . . , and Miss Hunter often told Nicky: "I'm going to put you in . . .!" And she did! Nicky is . . . and passes on . . . ! She even opens . . . sometimes! As you can imagine, Nicky isn't . . . about all this!

G Vocabulary practice. Complete these sentences, using the words in the box.

| artist | cafe | funny | greengrocer's | opposite |
| borrow | detective | gossip | hobbies | supermarket |

1 Can I . . . one of your books? A . . . story, maybe.
2 Do we really need to go to the baker's *and* the . . . ? We can get everything at the . . . , can't we?
3 Let's meet in the . . . next to the bookshop. Then you can tell me all the latest . . . !
4 Do you have any . . . ? Well, I do paint a little, but I'm not exactly an . . . !
5 Who's that . . . looking man who lives . . . the chemist's? I'm just curious, that's all!

H Discussion

Miss Hunter wrote detective stories. Have you ever written a story? Did you write about real people? If you were a writer, what sort of books would you like to write?

17

Read and decide. Mrs Wood won some money. 1) How? 2) How much? 3) Did she give the money to her family?

When a cheque for £200,000 arrived in the post one morning, Mrs Wood nearly fainted. She did the football pools every week, but she never expected to win anything. She never mentioned it to her family because she did not want them to laugh at her. Her husband and her son Ron knew all about football.
5 They did the pools every week too and quite often won a few pounds.

The family was in the kitchen when she came in holding the cheque, unable to say a word. Her husband took the cheque from her and put it in the middle of the kitchen table. Her son made her sit down and her daughter Diane gave her a cup of tea. Two hundred thousand pounds! They forgot all about Mrs
10 Wood and began to argue about the money.

"Well, I'll be able to give up my job at last and stay at home," said Mr Wood. He was fifty-two and worked as a lorry driver. "We'll buy a nice house in the country, a new car – and have a nice easy life!"

"Don't be selfish, Dad!" exclaimed Ron. "You're old – you don't need the
15 money! There's nothing wrong with this house and you've got a car already. No, I have a different idea. We'll start a business – something in computers or video. I'll run it and you can help. And we'll all share the profits."

"Just listen to you!" Diane said. "You're just as selfish as Dad! And you're both stupid! This money won't do us any good... can't you see that? It'll ruin
20 our lives. Money always ruins people's lives. The best thing to do is to send the cheque back, or else give it to charity."

Then a real argument broke out. It went on and on until a voice interrupted them. "Stop it, all of you!" It was Mrs Wood, with a determined look on her face. "Now listen to me," she said, standing up. "You've all forgotten some-
25 thing, haven't you? This is *my* money, not *yours*. *I* won it and *I'm* going to spend it. Of course I'll give you all a share. After all, you are my family! But *I'll* make the decisions! Is that clear?"

Mrs Wood picked up the cheque and put it in her pocket. Then, without saying another word, she walked out of the room.

A Find these words and phrases in the text:
fainted (*line 2*); give up my job (*line 11*); selfish (*line 14*);
charity (*line 21*); broke out (*line 22*); determined (*line 23*).

Now choose the right meaning.
1 stop working
2 thinking only of oneself
3 fell down unconscious
4 firm
5 a group doing good work for others
6 began

B Choose the right answer.

1 When Mrs Wood won the football pools: a) she was afraid to tell her family b) she couldn't believe it c) she didn't want the money
2 Mrs Wood's family forgot all about her because: a) she couldn't speak b) they were only interested in the money c) she was drinking her tea
3 Diane did not want to keep the money because she thought: a) it was bad for them b) it was not for them c) her family was stupid
4 In the end Mrs Wood decided to: a) throw the cheque away b) spend the money herself c) give the money away

C Give the words or phrases for these pronouns.

1 Mrs Wood got *one* in the post.
2 Diane gave her mother *one*.
3 Mr Wood worked as *one*.
4 Mr Wood wanted to buy *one* in the country.
5 Ron wanted to start *one*.

D Answer these questions.

1 How much did Mrs Wood win?
2 Did Mrs Wood know anything about football?
3 Where did Mrs Wood go with the cheque?
4 Did Mr Wood want to spend the money?
5 Did Ron agree with his father?
6 Did Diane want to start a business?
7 Did Mrs Wood argue with her family?
8 What did Mrs Wood do with the cheque?
9 Where did Mrs Wood go?
10 Did Mrs Wood's family say anything?

E Put these sentences in order.

1 Mrs Wood interrupted the argument.
2 Mr Wood took the cheque from his wife.
3 Mrs Wood went out of the kitchen.
4 Ron made his mother sit down.
5 Mrs Wood told her family it was her money.
6 Mrs Wood came into the kitchen with the cheque.
7 Mrs Wood picked up the cheque.
8 The family began to argue about the money.
9 Diane gave her mother a cup of tea.

F Guided composition. Complete this paragraph.

When Mrs Wood won . . . on the . . . , everyone in her . . . knew how to spend it for her! Her . . . wanted to give up his . . . , buy a . . . in the . . . and live a . . . . Her . . . wanted to start a . . . in . . . or . . . . Her . . . wanted to send the . . . back or else give it to . . . . Unfortunately, they all forgot about Mrs Wood herself! She told them that it was her . . . and, although she was going to give them all a . . . , she was going to make the . . . .

G Vocabulary practice. Complete these sentences, using the words in the box.

| argument | cheque | interrupt | ruined | video |
| business | decisions | profits | share | won |

1 I think she was completely selfish! She . . . a lot of money and didn't give anyone a . . . !
2 You'd better not start a . . . . You won't be any good at it. You don't like making . . . .
3 With that . . . for £1000 you could buy a . . . if you liked.
4 I think we'd better . . . them before a real . . . breaks out!
5 He spent all the . . . and . . . a perfectly good business.

H Discussion

Have you ever won any money? How? What would you do with a lot of money if you won it?

18

Read and decide. How would you describe Ron's journey?
a) boring b) unpleasant c) unhappy

24 Park Road   May 10
London S10

Dear Pat,

Some time ago I asked you about the best way to travel to Edinburgh overnight and you advised me to go by coach. "It's cheap and convenient," you said. "And very comfortable." Well, I took your advice. Now let me tell you what happened!

5. We left on time (and with plenty of loud music!) and stopped for supper at a cafe at about 9.30. It wasn't the sort of place I like eating in and it was also very crowded, so I decided to buy some chocolate. I had some fruit with me too, so at least I didn't go hungry.

We set off again at 10.15. The lights went off (and the awful music too, thank
10 goodness) and I settled down to get some sleep. However, the people just behind me kept on talking and every now and then they burst out laughing at some joke. I asked them to be quiet, but they didn't take any notice at all. However, eventually I fell asleep – but then the people behind me woke me up! "You're snoring," they said, "and keeping us awake!" After that I hardly
15 slept at all.

The rest of the journey was like a long bad dream. Then, at about 5.30, about 40 miles south of Edinburgh, the coach broke down. The driver went off to telephone for help, but when a rescue van finally arrived, they couldn't get the coach to start. In the end, they had to send for another one and we
20 all had to change coaches – in the rain! By that time I was very hungry and I was longing for a nice hot drink. I got one – when we finally reached Edinburgh at nine o'clock! By then I was so exhausted I went straight to bed and stayed there for the rest of the day – the first day of my holiday!

As you can imagine, I don't intend to travel by coach again overnight. Of
25 course I'm not blaming you for all this – but thanks for the advice!

Yours,
Ron

A Find these words and phrases in the text:

took your advice (*line 3*); set off (*line 9*); settled down (*line 10*);
broke down (*line 17*); rescue (*van*) (*line 18*); longing for (*line 21*).

Now choose the right meaning.

1 made (myself) comfortable
2 (van) to help them
3 did what you said
4 left
5 wanting very much
6 stopped going

B Choose the right answer.

1 Ron didn't have supper in the cafe because: a) he wasn't hungry b) he had his own food c) he didn't like the cafe
2 Ron couldn't get to sleep on the coach because the people behind him: a) snored a lot b) made a lot of noise c) laughed at him
3 Ron arrived in Edinburgh: a) in a different coach b) in a van c) in the same coach
4 Ron spent the first day of his holiday: a) travelling b) looking for food c) sleeping

C Give the words or phrases for these pronouns.

1 Ron bought *some* at the cafe.
2 *It* went off after they left the cafe.
3 *It* came to help them.
4 Ron wanted *one* after they changed coaches.

D Make questions and answers.

Where When	did the coach	stop for supper? leave the cafe? break down? reach Edinburgh?

It	broke down at half past five. arrived there at nine o'clock. left at a quarter past ten. stopped at half past nine. broke down forty miles south of Edinburgh. stopped at a cafe.

E Which of these things annoyed Ron?

1 The coach left on time.
2 The cafe wasn't very good.
3 The music on the coach stopped when they left the cafe.

4 The people behind him made a lot of noise.
5 The people behind him woke him up.
6 The coach broke down.
7 They had to change coaches in the rain.
8 He got a hot drink in Edinburgh.
9 He had to spend the first day in bed.

F Guided composition. Complete this letter from a friend of Ron's.

Before you decide to travel overnight by coach, let me tell you what happened to a friend of mine recently. First of all, the people behind him . . . and, when he asked them . . . , they . . . . Then, when he finally . . . , they . . . because he . . . ! The result: he . . . . However, that wasn't all. In the early hours of the morning, the coach . . . . They couldn't get it . . . , so in the end they . . . . When this arrived, they all had to . . . ! Well, they eventually . . . at nine o'clock – and my friend . . . that he . . . ! Do you still want to travel by coach? Think again!

G Vocabulary practice. Complete these sentences, using the words in the box.

| break down | coach | in the end | longing for | overnight |
| chocolate | comfortable | keep on | notice | send for |

1 I'm sorry your journey wasn't very . . . – but please don't blame me! It wasn't my fault if the . . . was crowded.
2 Well, if you're going to travel . . . , you'd better take some . . . in case you get hungry.
3 Let's hope the car doesn't . . . ! We can't . . . help from here!
4 Take my advice! Don't take any . . . of them, even if they . . . laughing at you.
5 I'm . . . a holiday abroad, but . . . I'll probably just stay at home.

H Discussion

Ron had a bad experience when he travelled by coach. Have you ever travelled overnight by coach? Did you like it? Why (not)? What is your favourite way of travelling?

19

Read and decide. What was Rod's 'very strange experience'?

Rod always used to laugh at the idea of flying saucers. "If there are people in outer space," he used to say, "they won't want to come here, will they?"

But that was before Rod had a very strange experience....

One summer evening, just as he was getting ready to go to bed, Rod heard a
5 low humming noise outside, like thousands of bees. He looked out of his bedroom window. In the field at the end of the garden he saw a number of bright objects coming down. As they landed, their lights went out and the field became dark. Rod decided to take a closer look from the wall at the end of his garden.

10 From there he could see the mysterious objects quite clearly. There were twelve of them in all and they were long and thin, like enormous cigars. In the centre of the machines he could just make out a group of figures, all wearing space suits. They appeared to be having a meeting.

As he stood there, Rod felt sure that these men were from outer space.
15 Their machines were the famous flying saucers. Rod also felt sure that they came from a quiet, peaceful planet, quite unlike the world he lived in. And he wanted to join them!

At that moment the figures began to move back towards their machines. They went inside and the low humming noise began again. One by one the
20 machines lit up. Then the first machine rose into the air, spinning like a wheel. A second one followed it, and then a third....

Rod felt terribly sad. The machines were leaving without him! He jumped over the low wall. "Wait!" he shouted. "Take me with you! Please!" But as he rushed forward, a wave of hot air pushed him back and he fell to the
25 ground. When he opened his eyes, the field was empty.

Did he really see flying saucers or was it all a dream? Rod is not sure. But these days, when anyone mentions flying saucers, Rod keeps quiet. And he feels very sad, remembering the happy peaceful planet he wanted to go to.

A Find these words in the text:

mysterious (*line 10*); unlike (*line 16*); lit up (*line 20*); spinning (*line 20*); terribly (*line 22*).

Now choose the right meaning.
1 going round and round
2 became bright
3 very
4 strange
5 different from

60

B Choose the right answer.

1 Rod went to the end of the garden because he saw: a) some strange objects b) some bees c) some people
2 The figures in space suits were: a) standing together and talking b) smoking c) walking around
3 Rod jumped over the wall because he wanted to: a) examine the machines b) go away with the machines c) meet the people in space suits
4 As a result of his experience, Rod's ideas about flying saucers are: a) clearer b) more interesting c) different

C Ask and answer questions.

Why did Rod	look out of his bedroom window? go to the end of the garden? feel sad? jump over the wall? fall to the ground?

He wanted to leave with the machines.
A wave of hot air pushed him back.
The machines were leaving without him.
He wanted to see the machines more clearly.
He heard a low humming noise.

D Answer these questions. Where was Rod:

1 when he first heard the machines?
2 when the machines began to leave?
3 when he fell to the ground?

E Right or wrong?

1 Rod wasn't afraid of the mysterious objects.
2 The machines were still bright when Rod reached the end of the garden.
3 Rod counted the machines.
4 Rod spoke to the figures in space suits.
5 All the machines left at the same moment.
6 Rod tried to follow the machines.

F Guided composition. Complete this letter from Rod to a friend.

Why have I changed my mind about flying saucers? I'll tell you! It happened . . . . I was just . . . at the time. I heard . . . outside. It sounded like . . . ! I looked out of . . . and there, . . . , I saw . . . . I decided to . . . . When I got there, I could see . . . quite clearly: there were . . . ; they were . . . (just like big cigars!) and, . . . , there were some figures in . . . who seemed to be . . . . I felt quite sure that they . . . and I wanted . . . ! But I couldn't. The machines began to leave and, as I . . . , a wave of hot air . . . . When I . . . , the field . . . ! Perhaps I didn't really . . . , but I shall never forget . . . where I think those people lived!

G Vocabulary practice. Complete these sentences, using the words in the box.

bees	flying saucers	humming	meeting	rose
closer	gone out	outer space	mysterious	space suits

1 What's that . . . object in the field over there? Let's go and take a . . . look.
2 Can you hear a strange . . . noise? It sounds like hundreds of . . . .
3 If . . . really do exist, I don't think they come from . . . .
4 I think the . . . is over. Look, the lights have . . . and the building is in darkness.
5 One by one the figures in . . . went back to their machines. One by one the machines . . . into the air and vanished.

H Discussion

Do you believe in flying saucers? Why (not)? What do you know about them? Do you think that there are people on other planets?

20

Read and decide. How did Nick feel after his 'little adventure'?
a) pleased   b) worried   c) disappointed

Nick was bored with life. Every day was exactly the same. He got up at exactly the same time; he caught the same bus to work; he did the same things in the office; he talked to the same people; he came home at the same time; he watched the same programmes on television – and he went to bed at the same time!

"What I need is a little adventure!" Nick thought as he waited at the bus stop one morning. Nick's 'little adventure' happened sooner than he expected!

While he was on the bus, reading his newspaper (the same one that he read every morning), the man sitting next to him suddenly pushed a large brown envelope into his hands. "Here, take this!" he muttered. Then he stood up and got off the bus before Nick could say a word.

Nick sat there, holding the envelope. It felt heavy. There were papers inside, or money perhaps. "I'd better hand it over to the police," he thought. There was a police station close to his office. But, as he got off the bus, a man approached him. He was obviously waiting for something. "He wants the envelope," Nick thought. Nick began to walk quickly – and the man hurried after him. Nick started to run – and the man began to run too. But then, just before he got to the police station, Nick managed to lose the man in the crowds. When he entered the police station, the man was no longer in sight.

Inside the police station, Nick handed over the envelope to the inspector in charge. The inspector opened it. The envelope was full of money – false money. "Obviously the man made a mistake," the inspector said. "He thought you were one of the gang! Well, congratulations!"

Nick felt like a hero. He could already see his name in all the papers. He could imagine an interview on television!

"However," the inspector went on, interrupting Nick's daydreams, "I'm afraid I must ask you to keep quiet about all this. We're trying to catch some very clever thieves – and we don't want them to know that we have some of the money. So you mustn't say a word to anyone – not even your boss! Sorry!"

"So that's that!" Nick said to himself on his way to the office. He was over an hour late. "I've had my little adventure... but I can't tell anyone about it, so what's the point? I've even got to make up an excuse for the boss!"

A Find these words and phrases in the text:

muttered (*line 10*); no longer (*line 19*); in charge (*line 21*); congratulations (*line 23*); keep quiet (*line 27*); make up (*line 33*).

Now choose the right meaning.

1 who was most important
2 say nothing
3 said quietly
4 well done
5 no more
6 invent

B Choose the right answer.

1 Nick was bored because his life wasn't very: a) pleasant b) easy c) interesting
2 The man gave Nick an envelope while he was going: a) home b) to work c) to the bus stop
3 Nick decided to take the envelope to the police because he thought it was: a) dangerous b) heavy c) important
4 The man who wanted the envelope knew: a) the man on the bus b) Nick c) the police
5 After his adventure, Nick expected to be: a) rich b) important c) famous

C Give the words or phrases for these pronouns.

1 *He* made a mistake.
2 *He* tried to get the envelope from Nick.
3 *He* knew all about the thieves.
4 *He* was late for work.

D Answer these questions.

1 Where did Nick work?
2 How did Nick go to work?
3 What was Nick doing on the bus?
4 Did Nick know the man on the bus?
5 Did Nick open the envelope?
6 Did Nick run all the way to the police station?
7 Could Nick see the man when he entered the police station?
8 Was the inspector pleased with Nick?
9 Did the inspector give the money to Nick?
10 Did Nick appear on television?

E Match the statements in table I with those in table 2.

1

Nick did the same things every day.	1
A man gave Nick an envelope.	2
A man began to follow Nick.	3
The inspector congratulated Nick.	4
Nick couldn't talk about his adventure.	5

2

	pleased.	a
	surprised.	b
He was (probably)	bored.	c
	disappointed.	d
	afraid.	e

F Guided composition. Complete Nick's excuse to his boss by using the correct form of the verb in brackets.

As I . . . (*stand up*) . . . (*get off*) the bus this morning,
I . . . (*find*) a large brown envelope on the seat next to me. I couldn't remember who . . . (*sit*) there, but I . . . (*think*) it . . . (*be*) a young woman. The envelope . . . (*feel*) heavy: there . . . (*be*) obviously papers inside. But there . . . (*be*) no address on the envelope, so I . . . (*decide*) . . . it . . . (*hand over*) to the police. At the police station, the inspector in charge . . . (*open*) the envelope; there . . . (*be*) some very important papers inside – and the address of the woman's office. Of course she . . . (*want*) . . . (*thank*) me personally, so I . . . (*have to*) . . . (*wait*) until she . . . (*arrive*) in the inspector's office. That's why I'm so late!

G Vocabulary practice. Complete these sentences, using the words in the box.

| boss | envelope | hand over | interview | police |
| congratulations | false | in charge of | papers | thieves |

1 That ring you found on the bus – you'd better . . . it . . . to the . . . .
2 I really enjoyed your . . . on television. . . .!
3 Who's . . . this office? I mean, who's the . . . here?
4 They've just caught that gang of . . . – the ones that made all that . . . money.
5 The . . . seemed quite heavy. In fact, when I opened it, it was full of old . . . !

H Discussion

Nick was bored with life. What can someone do to make life a little more exciting? Mention some jobs that you think are boring and others that you think are exciting.

21

> **Read and decide.** Did Tony (=the writer) enjoy his evening out?

It was my birthday last Thursday and I decided to celebrate it by inviting a few friends out to supper. I chose a restaurant in a quiet part of town. It is one of my favourite restaurants because the food is good and the waiters are friendly. It is hardly ever crowded, however, because few people know about
5 it, so it is not usually necessary to book a table. In any case, Thursday is not a busy evening as a rule.

When we entered the restaurant, I was surprised, therefore, to find it completely full. I looked around – but not a single table was free. One of the waiters recognised me. He came across and explained the situation. "A party
10 of tourists came in about half an hour ago," he said. "It was like an invasion! Suddenly the place was full! We can hardly manage!"

The waiter then pointed to a table in the corner. "The people there are just about to leave," he said. "Just hold on and you'll find a place there." He was right. Fifteen minutes later, the people at the corner table paid their bill,
15 got up and left. I led my friends across and we all sat down.

Unfortunately, our table was almost out of sight. We tried to attract the attention of the waiter who sent us there but he, like all the other waiters, was busy with the party of tourists. They ordered enormous quantities of food. But at last, nearly an hour later, the tourists were finishing their meal and
20 looking very pleased with life. The waiter, now very tired, appeared at our table. I advised my friends about the best dishes and finally the waiter went off with our order.

A few moments later he came back to our table. We could tell from his face that he had bad news for us. Full of apologies, he informed us that there
25 was no meat or fish left. "All we can offer you," he said, "is an omelette!"

A Find these words and phrases in the text:

celebrate (*line 1*); as a rule (*line 6*); recognised (*line 9*); about to (*line 13*); hold on (*line 13*); quantities (*line 18*); full of apologies (*line 24*).

Now choose the right meaning.
1 amounts
2 knew
3 make it a happy occasion
4 wait
5 usually
6 saying (he) was sorry
7 going to

B Try to guess the meaning of these words.

1 crowded (*line 4*)   3 informed (*line 24*)
2 enormous (*line 18*)

C Say why:

1 Tony invited some friends out to supper.
2 Tony chose that restaurant.
3 The restaurant was full that evening.
4 Tony and his friends were able to get a table after fifteen minutes.
5 The waiter didn't come to their table for nearly an hour.
6 Tony was able to advise his friends about the food.
7 The waiter who took their order came back and apologised.

D Answer these questions. If you cannot find the answer in the text, say: "The answer isn't there."

1 Where was the restaurant?
2 Was the restaurant very big?
3 Was the restaurant cheap?
4 Did Tony book a table?
5 Were the tourists already in the restaurant when Tony arrived?
6 Did all the tourists come at the same time?
7 Did the tourists eat a lot?
8 What did the tourists eat?
9 Did the tourists enjoy their meal?
10 Did Tony and his friends want to eat omelettes?

E Complete these sentences. Use the ideas in the text.

1 Tony did not . . . because the restaurant was . . . .
2 "You'll soon . . . over there," the waiter said, pointing to . . . .
3 Tony tried to . . . of one of the waiters, but he . . . .
4 The waiter stood near their table while Tony . . . .
5 "I'm . . . ," the waiter said when he came back. "There's . . . . We can only . . . !"

F Make 2–3 sentences about each of the following.

1 the restaurant
2 the tourists

G Guided composition. Complete this paragraph.

I went out with Tony the other evening. It was his birthday, so he . . . . He probably expected to find it empty. Instead, ... We had to wait . . . before we . . . . And then we had to

67

wait ... before a waiter .... Of course Tony then spent a long time .... Eventually the waiter .... almost immediately. "Sorry!" he said. " ... !" Omelette is not one of my favourite dishes!

H Vocabulary practice. Complete these sentences, using the words in the box.

apology	bill	celebrate	news	restaurant
as a rule	birthday	friendly	recognise	tourists

1 Did you say it was your ... ? Well, in that case let's ... by going out to supper!
2 It's strange. The place is full of ... tonight. ..., there isn't a single person here.
3 Do you ... that man in the corner – the one who's just paying his ... ?
4 I've got some bad ... for you. That ... I mentioned isn't open on Sundays.
5 He wasn't very .... He didn't even offer an ... !

I Discussion

Have you got a favourite restaurant or cafe? Where is it? How often do you go there? Why do you like it?

22

Read and decide. Sandra has some problems. Does Mrs MacDonald agree to help with all of them?

27 Barnes Avenue, London W.10   March 1st

Dear Mrs MacDonald,

As you know, we've been in the flat now for six months. We like it, but I'm afraid there are a few problems.

First, a good deal of the furniture is rather old. The armchairs, for example, are in bad condition and so is the big table where we eat. Could you please replace these items?

Secondly, the flat is extremely cold in winter. The central heating doesn't work very well and we have to use electric fires. And *they* are expensive, of course. Part of the problem is the windows. They don't fit very well, so they let the wind in.

Finally, there's the kitchen. It really does need painting. We are quite prepared to do the work ourselves if you pay for the paint.

Can you possibly come and look at the flat yourself? I'm sure you will agree with us. In any case, please let us know about these things as soon as possible.

                                       Yours sincerely,
                                       Sandra Shaw

19 Burns Avenue, Peebles, Scotland   March 18th.

Dear Ms Shaw,

Thank you for your letter. I'm sorry to hear you're having problems with the flat. I can't solve them all, of course, but I'll try to be helpful.

1 *Furniture* You liked it when you moved in! You told me so! But now you've changed your mind. Well, I'm sorry I can't help you there.

2 *Heating* I agree the flat can be cold in winter. I lived there myself for twenty years, so I know! But I always used electric fires and I'm afraid you must do the same. But get someone to look at the windows, by all means.

3 *Kitchen* Yes, it probably does need painting. Your idea is a good one. Please buy the paint and send me the bill. But make sure you choose a suitable colour (nothing too 'modern', please). And why not do the bathroom at the same time?

I'm sorry I can't come to inspect the flat personally, but I do live rather a long way off, you know.

                                       Yours sincerely,
                                       Janet MacDonald

A Find these words and phrases in the text:

a good deal of (*line 5*); don't fit very well (*line 10*); solve (*line 21*); by all means (*line 26*); suitable (*line 28*); inspect (*line 31*).

Now choose the right meaning.

1 are the wrong size
2 right for (the place)
3 much of
4 certainly
5 find the answer to
6 look at carefully

B Try to guess the meaning of these words.

1 replace (*line 7*)
2 prepared to (*line 13*)
3 bill (*line 28*)

C Say why:

1 Sandra is writing to Mrs MacDonald.
2 Sandra wants new armchairs.
3 Sandra has to use electric fires.
4 Sandra does not want to use electric fires.
5 The windows let the wind into the flat.

D Which of these things is Mrs MacDonald willing to help with?

1 central heating
2 the kitchen
3 the armchairs
4 the windows
5 the big table

E Answer these questions. If you cannot find the answer in the text, say: "The answer isn't there."

1 Does Sandra live alone in the flat?
2 Does Sandra want to leave the flat?
3 How big is the flat?
4 Is all the furniture old?
5 Which room needs repainting?
6 Is Sandra willing to pay for the paint?
7 How long did Mrs MacDonald live in the flat?
8 When did she leave the flat?
9 Does Mrs MacDonald want to spend a lot of money on the flat?
10 Is Mrs MacDonald coming to London to see the flat?

F Complete these sentences. Use the ideas in the text.

1 Both . . . and . . . are in bad condition.
2 The flat is extremely cold in winter, partly because . . . and partly because . . . .

3 You actually told me that you ... when you moved into the flat!
4 When I lived ... myself, I always used ....
5 When you ... the kitchen, why not ... too?

G Give more details.

1 Could you please replace *these items*?
2 We are quite prepared to do *the work* ourselves.
3 I'm afraid you must do *the same*.
4 *Your idea* is a good one.

H Guided composition. Complete Sandra's reply to Mrs MacDonald's letter.

Thank you for your letter of March 18th.
First, the furniture: perhaps I did say I ... but it was a very dark day so I could not ...! Anyway, I certainly ... now!
Secondly, the heating: of course I will get someone to ... but I must also get someone to ... too. As I said in my letter, it doesn't ....
If we stay, we will certainly paint ..., but we are not prepared to ... at the same time!
Please think about our problems again, otherwise I'm afraid ....

I Vocabulary practice. Complete these sentences, using the words in the box.

| central heating | electric | modern | problems | suitable |
| condition | | mind | prepared | replacing | work |

1 That ... fire is no use. It doesn't ... properly.
2 That ... furniture isn't really ... for this old flat.
3 The ... is a bit of a problem. It's in such bad ....
4 You offered to help me solve some of these .... Why did you change your ...?
5 The whole house needs painting and most of the furniture needs .... Are you ... to pay for it?

J Discussion

Do you think that Mrs MacDonald is a bad landlady? What would you do if you were Sandra? Do you think that Sandra stayed in the flat?

23

> **Read and decide.** Ben (= the writer) mentions an event which the interviewer recognises. What is it?

The interviewer led me into a small room next to the TV studio and gestured towards an armchair. "Take a seat," he said. "I've sent for some coffee. It'll be here in a moment."

He was a tall young man, thin, with dark glasses and longish hair. He wore old jeans and an Indian style shirt.

"Right," he said, sitting down opposite me and opening a notebook. "Let me tell you something about the programme. I'll begin by introducing you – and saying a few nice words about you! Then we'll start talking. Most of the time I'll ask questions, but if you like, you can just keep on talking. OK?"

"OK!" I said.

"Well now, let's see. I need to check a few facts with you. You were born in Dublin – when was it? – thirty seven years ago. You went to university in England – in London. But you didn't take a degree, I see. Why was that?"

"Oh, I got bored," I explained. "I didn't like spending all my time in libraries and lecture rooms. I wanted to *do* something!"

"So what *did* you do exactly?" the interviewer asked.

"Well, I got a job as a steward on one of the boats that went between England and Australia – for tourists and immigrants. I used to be away for about three months at a time and then we got six weeks' leave in England. It was during one of these 'rest periods' in England that I wrote my first book – a collection of short stories. I did it mainly to pass the time! 'Below Decks', I called it. Have you read it?"

The interviewer shook his head. "I'm afraid not," he said. "I haven't been able to get hold of a copy. Anyway, I suppose it was about your life as a steward, to judge from the title?"

"That's right" I said. "It was a comic book, mainly, because – as you can imagine – lots of funny things used to happen on board ship. But it wasn't all fun. Once the ship caught fire and that was really quite serious. We had to get all the passengers off, although we saved the ship in the end."

The interviewer stared at me. "That was near Mombasa, wasn't it?" he asked.

"Yes," I told him. "But you haven't read the book – so how do you know? Did you see the film?"

"No," he told me. "It just happens that I was on that boat! I was a child at the time and I was coming back from Australia with my parents. For us kids that fire was the one exciting thing that happened during the voyage! Well, what a coincidence! I must write and tell my mother all about you!"

A **Find these words in the text:**

gestured (*line 1*); steward (*line 17*); leave (*line 19*); judge (*line 25*); comic (*line 26*); coincidence (*line 37*).

Now choose the right meaning.

1 decide
2 holiday
3 pointed
4 strange event
5 funny
6 kind of waiter

B **Try to guess the meaning of these words and phrases.**

1 take a seat (*line 2*)
2 keep on (*line 9*)
3 stared (*line 30*)

C **Say where:**

1 Ben was born.
2 Ben went to university.
3 Ben worked as a steward.
4 Ben wrote his first book.
5 Ben helped to save the passengers on a ship.

D **Answer these questions. If you cannot find the answer in the text, say: "The answer isn't there."**

1 What was the interviewer wearing?
2 Did the interviewer know anything about Ben already?
3 How old was Ben?
4 Was the interviewer younger than Ben?
5 Did Ben enjoy being at university?
6 Did Ben enjoy working as a steward?
7 Did Ben have any leave in Australia?
8 What was Ben's first book about?
9 Was Ben's first book successful?
10 Why did the interviewer remember the fire on the ship?

E **Complete these sentences. Use the ideas in the text.**

1 The interview took place in . . . .
2 First of all the interviewer . . . . Then he checked . . . .
3 The interviewer wanted to know what . . . after he left university.
4 The interviewer wanted to read . . . , but he couldn't . . . .
5 The interviewer knew all about . . . because he happened to . . . .

73

F Make true sentences and then put them in order.

The interviewer Ben	described his first book. checked some facts. discovered he was a passenger on the same boat. talked about the programme. talked about his first job.	1 2 3 4 5

G Guided composition. Complete this letter. It is from the interviewer to his mother.

A very strange thing happened the other day. I was interviewing . . . called Ben Kelly, who many years ago . . . called 'Below Decks'. It was about his life as . . ., which were mainly full of . . . . Anyway, quite by chance, he mentioned that the ship he was working on . . . ! Of course I don't need to tell you anything more, because . . . , weren't we? I remember it very clearly because it was . . . . By the way, I haven't got . . . , but I'll send you mine as soon as I . . . one.

H Vocabulary practice. Complete these sentences, using the words in the box.

caught	collection	introduce	lecture	serious
coincidence	glasses	kids	library	style

1 What a . . . ! Your shirt is exactly the same . . . as mine!
2 But then the studio . . . fire – and that was more . . . .
3 What are all those . . . doing in the . . . room? They aren't students!
4 Can you . . . me to that tall man in dark . . . over there. I must meet him!
5 There's an extremely interesting . . . of old books in the . . . .

I Discussion

Ben worked on a boat as a steward. Would you like to do this for a time? Why (not)? Imagine that you want to write a book about your life. What sort of job would *you* choose?

24

Read and decide.
1) What part did Aunt Jane get in a film?
2) Did she ever see herself in the film?

Aunt Jane is now well over seventy, but she is still a great cinema-goer. The cinema in our town closed down years ago and sometimes she has to travel twenty miles or more to see a good film. And once a month at least she goes up to London to see the latest foreign films. Of course she could see most of these films on television, but the idea does not attract her. "It isn't the same," she says. "For one thing, the screen's too small. Besides, I like going to the cinema!"

One thing has always puzzled us. Although Aunt Jane has lots of friends and enjoys company, she always goes to the cinema alone. We discovered the reason for this only recently – from mother. "It may surprise you to learn that Aunt Jane wanted to be an actress when she was young," she told us. "She used to wait outside film studios all day, just to appear in crowd scenes. Your aunt has probably appeared in dozens of films – as a face in the crowd at a railway station or in the street! Sometimes she did not even know the name of the film they were making, so she couldn't go to see herself at the cinema!

"All the time, of course, she was looking for a small part in a film. Her big chance came when they started to make a film in our town. Jane managed to meet the director at a party, and he offered her a role as a shopkeeper. It really was a very small part – she only had a few lines to say – but it was an important moment for Jane. Before the great event, she rehearsed for days. In fact, she turned the sitting-room into a shop! We all had to help, going in and out of the shop until she was word perfect. And on the actual day she was marvellous. The director congratulated her. Jane thought that this was the beginning of her film career!

"Unfortunately, in the end, they did not include the shop scene in the film. But nobody told Jane! When the film first appeared in London, she took all her friends to see it. And of course she wasn't in it! It was a terrible blow! She stopped going to film studios and gave up the idea of becoming an actress. She still loves the cinema, as you all know, but from that day she has always gone alone!"

A Find these words and phrases in the text:

well over (*line 1*); company (*line 9*); studios (*line 12*); role (*line 18*); rehearsed (*line 20*); turned into (*line 21*); blow (*line 27*).

Now choose the right meaning.

1 disappointment
2 part in film or play
3 practised
4 being with people
5 made into
6 much more than
7 where films are made

B Try to guess the meaning of these words and phrases.

1 the idea does not attract her (*line 5*)
2 one thing has always puzzled us (*line 8*)
3 congratulated (*line 23*)
4 gave up the idea (*line 28*)

C Say why:

1 Aunt Jane does not like watching films on television.
2 Aunt Jane used to wait outside studios.
3 Aunt Jane couldn't go to see herself in films she appeared in.
4 Aunt Jane prepared very carefully for her role as shopkeeper.
5 Aunt Jane believed that she was going to be an actress at last.
6 Aunt Jane stopped going to film studios.

D Answer these questions. If you cannot find the answer in the text, say: "The answer isn't there."

Jane got a part in a film . . .

1 Was this the first time Jane appeared in a film?
2 Where were they making the film?
3 What was the name of the film?
4 What was the film about?
5 How did Jane get the part?
6 What did Jane have to do in the film?
7 Was it a big part?
8 Did Jane's family help her?
9 Did everyone enjoy helping Jane?
10 Was the director pleased with Jane?
11 Did Jane go to see the film?
12 Did Jane enjoy the film?

E Complete these sentences. Use the ideas in the text.

1 Aunt Jane often . . . to see a good film because there isn't . . .
2 Aunt Jane doesn't like watching films on TV partly because . . . and partly because . . . .
3 When she was young, Aunt Jane wanted to . . . , so she . . . all day.

4 Aunt Jane only had ..., but she ... until she was word perfect.
5 Aunt Jane ... to see the film when it appeared in London, but ... in it!

F Guided composition. Complete Jane's diary.

June 1   My big chance has come at last! They have ... in our town! I must ...!

June 8   I'm going to a party tomorrow. They say .... I must meet him.

June 10 I went to the party last night. I ... and he ... – as a shopkeeper! I only ... but that isn't important. This is my great chance!

June 20 I've ... for days! Everyone in the family .... We have even ... into a shop!

June 25 Today was the great day. Everyone says I ... and the director ... too! I really think this ... – at last!

G Vocabulary practice. Complete these sentences, using the words in the box.

blow	chance	foreign	parties	turned into
career	crowd	part	rehearse	well over

1 There were some fantastic ... scenes in the film, with ... ten thousand people in each!
2 When the business closed down, that was the end of his .... It was a terrible ... to him.
3 They offered me a ... in the play, but I really haven't time to ...
4 I like going to .... Besides, it's my only ... to meet interesting people.
5 Do you remember that cinema where they used to show ... films? Well, they've ... it ... a supermarket!

H Discussion

Jane wanted a part in a film. Would you like to be in a film too? Choose a role (big or small) which you think you could play.

25

Read and decide. Why is Jan in hospital?

St John's Hospital
Montreal

June 25th

Dear Ellen,

Well, I promised to write to you while I was on holiday but, honestly, I didn't expect to write to you from hospital! Perhaps I had better explain!

I went to the conference last week. Most of it was boring, but I met a few interesting (and pleasant!) people. As usual, we all ate too much and didn't get
5 enough sleep, so by the end of the week I was ready for a holiday – and a rest!

A friend lent me a small house in the hills for a few days. The place is about sixty miles from Montreal, and quite isolated – just trees, birds and small animals. I went by car and took plenty of food with me.

10 I slept well that night and got up bright and early the following morning, intending to go for a long walk. However, in a shed behind the house, I discovered a very old bicycle. "A good way to see the countryside," I thought as I set off after breakfast.

Everything went well for the first ten miles. Then I came to a steep hill.
15 Well, I managed to reach the top without getting off my bike (much to my surprise!) and began to go downhill. And then the trouble started! The brakes didn't work! I tried them again and again, but it was no use. I felt really scared, I can tell you. I kept on trying the brakes – and suddenly they *did* work! Of course by this time I was going much too fast and I shot off the bike into some
20 bushes. I broke my left arm, injured my shoulder and I have cuts and bruises all over. I was lucky I didn't break my neck! Otherwise, I'm all right! In a few days I shall be out of hospital and on my way home. But it hasn't been much of a holiday! Don't send any flowers or chocolates, but come and meet me at the airport if you like.

Love,
Jan.

PS I'm arriving on Monday July 9 on Flight AC 866 from Montreal.

A Find these words and phrases in the text:

honestly (*line 1*); conference (*line 3*); steep (*line 14*); brakes (*line 16*); didn't work (*line 17*); shot off (*line 19*); break my neck (*line 21*).

Now choose the right meaning.

1 meeting
2 did not stop the bike
3 kill myself
4 high
5 to tell the truth
6 fell off suddenly
7 something to make the bike stop

B   Try to guess the meaning of these words and phrases.

1 isolated (*line 8*)
2 bright and early (*line 10*)
3 shed (*line 11*)
4 kept on (trying) (*line 18*)

C   Say where:

1 Jan went to a conference.
2 Jan went to stay after the conference.
3 Jan found a bicycle.
4 Jan fell off the bicycle.
5 Jan spent most of her holiday.

D   Answer these questions. If you cannot find the answer in the text, say: "The answer isn't there."

1 Was Ellen expecting to get a letter from Jan?
2 Did Jan enjoy the conference?
3 How long was the conference?
4 What was the conference about?
5 Who lent Jan a house?
6 How long did Jan intend to stay in the house?
7 How did Jan get to the house?
8 Did Jan go to the house alone?
9 Why did Jan go out on the bike?
10 What was the bike like?
11 Did Jan go far on the bike?
12 What was wrong with the bike?
13 Did Jan hurt herself when she fell off the bike?
14 Has Jan got to stay much longer in hospital?
15 Has Jan enjoyed her holiday?

E   Complete these sentences. Use the ideas in the text.

1 After the conference, Jan went to stay . . . about . . . from Montreal.
2 Instead of . . . , as she intended, Jan went for a ride on . . . .
3 Although . . . , Jan did not have to . . . while she was going uphill.
4 When she discovered that . . . , Jan was really scared.
5 Jan was going so fast when the brakes . . . that she . . . .

F Give more details about:

1 the house Jan stayed in.
2 Jan's injuries.

G Guided composition. Complete this letter which Ellen wrote to a friend about Jan.

Begin like this:
Have you heard the news about Jan? As you remember, she went to that conference in Montreal. After the conference, . . .

Say: – *where Jan went*
– *what she did the next day*
– *what happened while she was going downhill*
– *where she is now*

End like this:
So, as you can see, she hasn't had much of a holiday! She's flying back on July 9. Why not come to the airport to meet her?

H Vocabulary practice. Complete these sentences, using the words in the box.

| brakes | bright and early | countryside | isolated | steep |
| break | conference | getting off | scared | surprise |

1 Were you very . . . when you found that the . . . of the car weren't working?
2 The hill's too . . . . We'll never get to the top without . . . our bikes.
3 I like the . . . , but I must admit that our house is rather . . . .
4 I didn't get half enough sleep during the . . . , so of course I never managed to wake up . . . !
5 Much to his . . . , he didn't . . . his leg. He only injured it.

I Discussion

Jan had a very unpleasant experience on her bike. Has anything like this ever happened to you?

80

26

Read and decide. 1) What was Andy's favourite TV programme? 2) Was he able to watch it on Friday evening?

Andy Barton was in a bad mood. It was Friday, and at six o'clock his favourite programme, *Travel with us*, was on TV. Andy liked to get home in good time for that. But then, just as he was leaving the office a little early, a customer rang up with a few complaints. The customer complained steadily for the next
5 fifteen minutes! "I can still get home in time if I hurry," Andy told himself as he dashed out of the office. But then, as he drove off in his car, he noticed that he was almost out of petrol. "I'll have to stop at Fenton's," Andy thought. He hated Fenton's because it was a self-service petrol station. "You do all the work yourself, but you pay the same for the petrol," he used to grumble.

10 But at Fenton's things went wrong again! The pump was not working properly and it took ages to get petrol. It was four minutes to six by the time Andy jumped back into his car and drove off. But at two minutes past six he was sitting in front of the television, watching *Travel with us*. He was on his way to Japan!

15 Then the phone rang. "Shall I answer it?" Andy thought. He tried to concentrate on Japan and forget the phone. But it kept on ringing and finally he picked it up.
"Mr Barton?" a voice said. "Fenton's Garage here."
"Fenton's?" said Andy. "Why, I was at your place only a few minutes ago,
20 getting some petrol. Did I leave something behind or what?" "No, you didn't, Mr Barton," the voice went on. "That's just the trouble! You didn't leave anything behind! You went off without paying for your petrol, you see! Now normally, when that happens, we ring up the police. But luckily I recognised you because I live in the same street as you, and I knew it was a mistake."
25 "I'm really very sorry," Andy said.
"Oh, that's all right, Mr Barton. These things happen! But could you come round now and pay for your petrol? And please hurry! We close at half past six!"

A Find these words and phrases in the text:

in a bad mood (*line 1*); steadily (*line 4*); ages (*line 11*); concentrate on (*line 16*); normally (*line 23*).

Now choose the right meaning.
1 pay attention to
2 generally
3 without stopping
4 annoyed
5 a long time

81

B   Try to guess the meaning of these words and phrases.

1 in good time (*line 2*)
2 dashed (*line 6*)
3 almost out of (petrol) (*line 7*)
4 properly (*lines 10–11*)

C   Say why:

1 Andy was in a bad mood.
2 A customer rang Andy up.
3 Andy liked to get home early on Friday evenings.
4 Andy had to stop at Fenton's.
5 Andy didn't like self-service petrol stations.
6 It took Andy a long time to get petrol.
7 Andy didn't want to answer the phone.
8 The man at Fenton's Garage rang Andy up.
9 The man at Fenton's Garage recognised Andy.
10 Andy had to go back to Fenton's Garage.

D   Answer these questions. If you cannot find the answer in the text, say: "The answer isn't there."

1 Where did Andy work?
2 What was Andy's job?
3 What did the customer complain about?
4 Did Andy have any petrol when he drove off in his car?
5 When did Andy leave the petrol station?
6 What was the TV programme about?
7 Did Andy watch this programme often?
8 Did Andy know the man at Fenton's Garage?
9 Was the man at Fenton's Garage angry with Andy?
10 Did Andy want to go back to Fenton's Garage?

E   Complete these sentences. Use the ideas in the text.

1 Andy's ... was on TV every ... at ....
2 A customer ... so Andy couldn't ....
3 Although it took ... petrol, Andy ... just after six.
4 Andy was already ... when the phone ....
5 The man at Fenton's Garage asked Andy to ... before they closed at half past six.

F   Give more details.

1 Andy liked to get home in good time for *that*.
2 "I was at *your place* only a few minutes ago."
3 "*These things* happen!"

G Guided composition. Complete Andy's diary.

It's been a terrible evening! First of all, I got away from the office late because . . . . That put me in a really bad mood! Then, to make things worse, as I was driving off, ... But that wasn't all! Just as I started to watch *Travel with us*, ... Well, I had to go round and pay, of course, and by the time I got back, the programme was over!

H Vocabulary practice. Complete these sentences, using the words in the box.

| ages | concentrate | gone wrong | in good time | normally |
| complains | customers | hurry | mood | trouble |

1 Let's try to leave . . . . Then we won't have to . . . for once.
2 Are you in some sort of . . . ? You don't seem able to . . . on anything these days.
3 Why is he in such a bad . . . ? Do you think something has . . . in the office?
4 She's one of our best . . . , but I don't like her. She . . . too much!
5 We're lucky tonight. . . . it takes . . . to get home at this time.

Discussion

Andy's favourite TV programme was *Travel with us*. What is your favourite programme? How often is it on? Do you hurry home (or stay at home) just to watch it?

27

> **Read and decide.** Dr Allen was 'in two places at once'.
> 1) What were the two places? 2) How was this possible?

The phone rang on Dr Allen's desk.

"Hello," she said, picking up the phone. "Dr Allen here."

"Oh, good morning, Dr Allen," a voice said. "It's Jenny Anderson here, Professor Smith's secretary. It's about that meeting on Monday. You are definitely coming, aren't you?"

"The meeting. Yes, of course," Dr Allen said, looking in her diary. "It's at eleven, I see."

"Well, no. We had to change the time," Jenny Anderson said. "It's going to be at twelve. I'm sure I told you."

"But I've got a lecture at twelve," Dr Allen said.

"But surely you can cancel your lecture – just for once," Jenny Anderson suggested. "The meeting's very important, as you know."

"I've never cancelled a lecture in my life," Dr Allen told her. "Sorry!" There was a silence. "However," she went on, "I've got an idea. I've just got a new cassette recorder – rather a good one, in fact. I'll record my lecture beforehand – and then I'll be able to come to the meeting."

"Wonderful," said Jenny Anderson. "I'll tell Professor Smith you'll be there, then."

At five to twelve on Monday morning Dr Allen went along to the lecture room. There were about twenty students waiting there for her. "I'm sorry," she told them, "I won't be able to give my lecture today." The students looked surprised. Dr Allen explained that she had an important meeting. "However," she went on, "although I can't be with you myself, my voice can!" She gestured towards the cassette recorder on the table. "You see, I've recorded my lecture and you can listen to it while I go to my meeting. So, in a way, I'll be in two places at once! One of the miracles of modern science!" Feeling rather pleased with herself, Dr Allen switched on the cassette recorder and left.

The meeting in Professor Smith's office finished a little early, so Dr Allen decided to go back to the lecture room. She stood for a moment outside the door, listening to her own voice. Then, very quietly, she opened the door. To her surprise, the room was empty. But then, as she looked around, she saw a number of of small cassette recorders – all 'listening' to her lecture!

"Well," she thought, "if I can be in two places at once, so can they!"

A Find these words in the text:

cancel (*line 11*); beforehand (*line 16*); miracle (*line 26*).

Now choose the right meaning.

1 earlier
2 wonderful event
3 not give

B Try to guess the meaning of these words.

1 definitely (*line 5*)
2 diary (*line 6*)
3 wonderful (*line 17*)
4 gestured (*line 23*)

C Give the words or phrases for these pronouns.

1 *It* was on Dr Allen's desk.
2 Jenny Anderson rang up about *it*.
3 Dr Allen didn't want to cancel *it*.
4 Dr Allen took *it* to the lecture room.
5 Dr Allen listened to *it* outside the door of the lecture room.

D Answer these questions. If you cannot find the answer in the text, say, "The answer isn't there."

1 Who was Jenny Anderson?
2 Why did she ring Dr Allen?
3 Did Dr Allen know about the meeting?
4 Where was the meeting?
5 What was the meeting about?
6 Who changed the time of the meeting?
7 Did Dr Allen want to cancel her lecture?
8 What was Dr Allen's 'idea'?
9 When did Dr Allen record her lecture?
10 When did Dr Allen go to the lecture room?
11 Were the students already in the lecture room?
12 Did Dr Allen tell the students about the meeting?
13 Did the students ask Dr Allen any questions?
14 Did the students listen to Dr Allen's lecture?
15 Where did the students go?
16 Was Dr Allen angry with the students?

E Find the original words.

1 Jenny Anderson wanted to know if Dr Allen was definitely coming to the meeting on Monday.
2 Jenny Anderson suggested that Dr Allen should cancel her lecture.
3 Dr Allen said that she would record her lecture beforehand and then she would be able to go to the meeting.
4 Dr Allen told the students that she wouldn't be able to give her lecture that day.

F Complete these sentences. Use the ideas in the text.

1 Dr Allen thought that . . . , but instead it was at twelve.
2 Jenny Anderson wanted . . . because the meeting was important.
3 Dr Allen . . . , so she was able to record her lecture beforehand.
4 Before she left the lecture room, Dr Allen . . . .
5 When she opened the door of the lecture room, Dr Allen expected to find . . . , not . . . !

G Guided composition. Complete this extract from a student's diary.

Today Dr Allen came into the lecture room and told us . . . . Of course we were all surprised because . . . . However, she went on to explain: " . . . ." Then, looking rather pleased with herself, ... Well, we've got cassette recorders too, so as soon as she left, we . . . !

H Vocabulary practice. Complete these sentences, using the words in the box.

| beforehand | cassette recorder | lecture | miracles | secretary |
| cancel | diary | meeting | record | switch on |

1 Can I borrow your . . . ? I want to . . . some music for the party.
2 What time is that . . . on space travel? Did you write it down in your . . . ?
3 Please . . . the electric heater in the office just before the . . . starts.
4 I'm afraid I had to . . . the meeting. Didn't my . . . inform you?
5 I don't believe in . . . ! It's much better to prepare everything carefully . . . .

I Discussion

Have you got a cassette recorder? Do you make recordings? (What of?) What kind of things *could* you record?

28

Read and decide.   Why did Tandem go back to his old school?

Tandem felt a little nervous as he entered the school gates. He was going back to his old school after twenty years and it was a very strange experience!

He crossed the school yard and walked towards the main entrance. He paused for a moment to examine the building. He could see his old classroom
5 on the first floor. It had a broken window. "It always had broken windows!" he thought.

Tandem pushed open the door and went in. It was exactly as he remembered it. The headmaster's study was on the left; the main staffroom was on the right. While he was standing there, the door of the staffroom opened and
10 two teachers came out. He caught a glimpse of the room inside. There were teachers standing near the fire, talking. Others were reading or correcting homework. Then the door closed again.

Tandem decided to have a quick look round the school before calling on the headmaster. He passed classroom after classroom. When he came to his old
15 classroom on the first floor, he paused for a moment. There was a lot of noise inside. "There was always a lot of noise!" he said to himself.

Next he came to the laboratories – physics, chemistry and biology. These were new. He could see the boys inside, busy with experiments. And finally he came to the library, where a few of the older boys were working quietly.
20 It all seemed so peaceful!

Then a bell rang and within seconds the corridor was full of noisy boys, all shouting and laughing. They were like a great flood, almost carrying Tandem along with them. He was glad when he finally reached the door of the headmaster's study.

25 He knocked at the door and waited. "Come in!" a voice called out. The headmaster stood up to greet him as he went in. He was an old man now and Tandem hardly recognised him.

"Good afternoon, Tandem," the headmaster said. "So you're an inspector now! Well, quite a few boys come back to visit their old school, but no one
30 has ever come back to inspect it before!"

A Find these words in the text:

staffroom (*line 8*); glimpse (*line 10*); experiments (*line 18*); flood (*line 22*); greet (*line 26*).

Now choose the right meaning.
1 welcome
2 a lot of moving water
3 quick look
4 trying to find something out
5 room for teachers

B Try to guess the meaning of these words.

1 nervous (*line 1*)   3 peaceful (*line 20*)
2 entrance (*line 3*)

C Say where:

1 Tandem paused for a moment.
2 There was a broken window.
3 Tandem went into the school.
4 Teachers were standing near the fire.
5 Boys were busy with experiments.
6 Boys were working quietly.
7 Boys were making a lot of noise.
8 Tandem met the headmaster.

D Make correct sentences.

Tandem	didn't go went	across along into past	the school yard. the headmaster's study. the staffroom. the corridor. his old classroom. the library. any of the classrooms.

E Answer these questions. If you cannot find the answer in the text, say: "The answer isn't there."

1 Why was Tandem nervous?
2 Did Tandem recognise his old classroom?
3 Were all the teachers in the staffroom talking?
4 Did the teachers in the staffroom see Tandem?
5 Was this the first time that Tandem saw the laboratories?
6 Were the boys in the laboratories working?
7 Were the boys in the library making any noise?
8 Did Tandem want to go into the library?
9 Why was Tandem glad to reach the headmaster's study?
10 Why was it difficult for Tandem to recognise the headmaster?

F Complete these sentences.

1 Before he entered the school, Tandem . . . to examine the building.
2 Through the open door . . . , Tandem could see . . . .

88

3 Everything was peaceful until . . . .
4 As he stood outside . . . , a voice called out, ". . . !"
5 "No one . . . before!" the headmaster told Tandem.

G Guided composition. Expand these notes that Tandem made about his visit to the school.

went back to my old school today – first visit for 20 years – very strange experience – walked round school – seemed much the same except for 3 new laboratories – stood outside old classroom (plenty of noise inside!) – stood outside library (boys working quietly there) – suddenly everything changed: bell rang and corridor full of boys – glad to get to headmaster's study!

H Vocabulary practice. Complete these sentences, using the words in the box.

broken	chemistry	entrance	experiments	greeting
building	corridor	examine	glimpse	study

1 If we wait near the . . . , maybe we'll catch a . . . of the director as he comes out.
2 I never liked . . . . I just wasn't any good at doing all those boring . . . in the laboratory!
3 Why don't we have a quick look round the . . . before we . . . it in detail?
4 Have you seen that . . . window in the headmaster's . . . ? Who did it, I wonder?
5 He passed us in the . . . without even . . . us!

I Discussion

Tandem went back to see his old school. Would you go back to see yours? What sort of changes would you like to find there?

89

29

> **Read and decide.** George (= the writer) lost something on the train. 1) What was it? 2) Did he find it?

We were lucky that morning. The train was not very crowded and we managed to get a corner seat to ourselves in one of those long open carriages. "I don't like this sort of carriage," Mark said as he took out papers for our meeting, "but at least you get a table to work on!" I fetched some coffee and biscuits from the restaurant car and we settled down to work. People passed up and down the train, and once the ticket inspector came to look at our tickets. But, apart from that, it was a peaceful journey.

"Good!" said Mark after an hour or so. "I think we've just about finished." He began to put away his papers. "What time is it?" he asked. "My watch has stopped." "About nine-thirty, I reckon," I said. "Hold on a moment. My watch is here somewhere on the table."

I looked under my own papers, and then on the floor, but there was no sign of my watch. It was not in my pockets, either.

"You didn't put it in your bag, did you?" I asked Mark. "Along with your papers." He checked, but the watch was not there.

"It's very odd," I said. "I remember taking it off and putting it on the table when we started work. No one's been near us except the ticket collector – and *he* didn't pick it up!"

"Someone came and cleared away the coffee cups," Mark said. "I remember seeing a man with a big plastic bag."

The man with the plastic bag came from the restaurant car, one of the passengers informed us. I went along there to see him and I explained my problem.

"Are you sure?" the man asked. "Look, there's the bag – full of rubbish. I don't want to empty everything out if you're not sure."

"I can't be absolutely certain," I said, "but my watch *was* on the table. I'll look in the bag myself if you like. It's a very expensive watch!"

"Well, in that case, we'd better have a look, sir," the man said and emptied everything out on the floor. There, among the paper coffee cups, half-eaten biscuits and pieces of paper, lay my very valuable watch!

"Phew!" I said. "I think I need another cup of coffee after that!"

"Sorry, sir," the man snapped. "The restaurant car is closed. We're almost at London."

A Find these words and phrases in the text:

apart from (*line 7*); or so (*line 8*); just about (*line 8*); odd (*line 16*); valuable (*line 30*).

Now choose the right meaning.

1 strange
2 worth a lot of money
3 about
4 almost
5 except for

B Try to guess the meaning of these words and phrases.

1 reckon (*line 10*)
2 hold on (*line 10*)
3 there was no sign of (*lines 12–13*)
4 cleared away (*line 19*)
5 rubbish (*line 24*)

C Say why:

1 George and Mark were able to work on the train.
2 George and Mark wanted to work on the train.
3 Mark asked George to tell him the time.
4 George looked in his pocket.
5 George went to the restaurant car.
6 The man in the restaurant car agreed to empty out the plastic bag.

D Answer these questions. If you cannot find the answer in the text, say: "The answer isn't there."

1 Where were George and Mark going?
2 Were there a lot of people on the train?
3 Did George and Mark have anything to eat before they started work?
4 How long did they work for?
5 Where did George look for his watch?
6 Who remembered seeing the man from the restaurant car?
7 What did the man from the restaurant car have with him?
8 Was the man from the restaurant car busy?
9 Did the man want to empty everything out of the plastic bag?
10 What other things were in the plastic bag?
11 Was George's watch dirty?
12 Did George get another cup of coffee?

E Give more details.

1 "I don't like *this sort of carriage*."
2 Apart from *that*, it was a peaceful journey.
3 "I remember seeing *a man with a big plastic bag*."
4 I explained *my problem*.

F Complete these sentences. Use the ideas in the text.

1 George and Mark worked for . . . . Then Mark began to . . . .
2 No one interrupted them on the train except for . . . , who . . . .
3 "Excuse me," George said to the man in the restaurant car, "I think . . . ."
4 George found his watch: it was lying . . . !
5 George wanted . . . at that moment, but he couldn't have one because . . . .

G Guided composition. Complete this extract from George's diary.

Begin like this:
I had a very unpleasant experience on the train this morning. I was travelling to London with Mark for a meeting. We had some coffee and biscuits and then . . .

Say: – *what you did on the train*
– *why you began to look for your watch*
– *why you decided to go to the restaurant car*
– *what happened in the restaurant car*

End like this:
The next time I have coffee and biscuits on the train I shall be more careful!

H Vocabulary practice. Complete these sentences, using the words in the box.

absolutely	clear away	plastic	restaurant car	ticket collector
carriage	fetch	problem	settle down	valuable

1 I'm not . . . certain, but I think there are seats in the next . . . .
2 If the . . . is still open, why don't you go and . . . some coffee?
3 How can it be . . . ? It's only made of . . . !
4 Let's . . . all these things. Then we can . . . to work properly.
5 Here comes the . . . ! You'd better try to explain your . . . to him.

I Discussion

George nearly lost something very valuable. Has this ever happened to you?

30

> **Read and decide.** How did Dick (= the writer) recognise his old jacket?

"It's silly," I told myself, as I tried to get some clothes into my crowded wardrobe. "I never wear half these things!" There were suits, jackets, trousers, shirts. Some were over ten years old. "I really must get rid of some of these," I decided. "Maybe I can get a few pounds for them."

5 I divided my clothes into three piles: those I wore regularly, those I hardly ever wore and, finally, those I never wore at all. I decided to get rid of all the things in the second and third piles and I put them into a suitcase.

But I couldn't make up my mind about one thing: an old grey jacket. I hardly ever wore it, but I liked it. It fitted me well and it looked smart. But it was 10 old, and there was a hole near one of the pockets. I tried to mend it, but the cotton I used was the wrong colour. So, in the end, I put the jacket into the suitcase along with the other clothes and set off to find a secondhand clothes shop. I found one near the town centre.

"It isn't easy to sell clothes like these," said the girl behind the counter. She 15 turned them over without much interest. "Still, I suppose I could give you ten pounds for the lot."

Ten pounds! It wasn't much for a suitcase of clothes. But in the end I left the shop with ten pounds in my pocket and an empty suitcase.

A few days later, my brother rang up. He asked if he could come and see 20 me. "I'd like you to meet a friend of mine," he said.

I did not care for my brother's friend. His name was Dennis and he liked talking. He knew about everything: cars and computers, art and sport; the latest films and the most recent books. As I listened to Dennis, I thought: "There's something familiar about you! Have we met before?" I tried hard to 25 remember. Then suddenly it became clear. It was not Dennis' face that was familiar. It was his jacket! He was wearing an old grey jacket – with a hole near one of the pockets!

"I like your jacket," I said to Dennis. "Very good cloth, I imagine."

"Yes," he said. "As a matter of fact I picked it up in a secondhand clothes 30 shop. It was a real bargain."

"How much did you pay for it?" I asked.

"Only ten pounds," he said. "It was cheap because of this hole near the pocket. Some fool tried to mend it – with the wrong colour cotton!"

Who did I hate more at that moment – Dennis or the girl in the shop? I 35 am still not sure!

A Find these words in the text:

piles (*line 5*); regularly (*line 5*); smart (*line 9*); familiar (*line 24*); picked up (*line 29*); bargain (*line 30*).

Now choose the right meaning:

1 got
2 (something) you recognise
3 very often
4 something very cheap
5 very nice
6 a number of things on top of one another

B Try to guess the meaning of these words.

1 wardrobe (*lines 1–2*)
2 suppose (*line 15*)
3 care for (*line 21*)
4 fool (*line 33*)

C Say why:

1 Dick decided to get rid of some of his clothes.
2 Dick couldn't make up his mind about the old grey jacket.
3 The girl in the secondhand clothes shop did not want to pay much for the clothes.
4 Dick didn't like Dennis very much.
5 Dick 'hated' Dennis.
6 Dick 'hated' the girl in the shop.

D Answer these questions. If you cannot find the answer in the text, say: "The answer isn't there."

1 Were all Dick's clothes old?
2 What was wrong with the grey jacket?
3 What colour cotton did Dick try to mend the jacket with?
4 Did Dick know where there was a secondhand clothes shop?
5 Was Dick hoping to get more than ten pounds for the clothes?
6 How did Dick spend the ten pounds?
7 Who was Dennis?
8 Did Dick enjoy listening to Dennis?
9 What was Dick doing while Dennis was talking?
10 Was Dennis pleased with the jacket?
11 How much did Dennis pay for the jacket?
12 Did Dick say to Dennis: "You're wearing my old jacket!"

E Complete these sentences. Use the ideas in the text.

1 Dick had so many clothes that it was difficult . . . .
2 Dick decided to get rid of the clothes he . . . and also the ones he . . . .

3 After trying to . . . , Dick put the jacket in the suitcase . . . .
4 " . . . ?" Dick's brother asked when he rang up.
5 According to Dennis, the person who . . . was a fool!

F Give more details.

1 I never wear half these *things*.
2 I divided my clothes into *three piles*.
3 He knew about *everything*.

G Guided composition. Complete this extract from Dick's brother's diary.

I took . . . last night and something very odd happened. It was clear from the start that Dick . . . (and I must admit that Dennis thinks he knows about everything: . . . !). Anyway, while Dick listened, he kept on . . . as if he was trying to . . . . Then suddenly they began talking about . . . – the one he picked up . . . the other day. Dennis said he got it cheap because . . . ! Dick looked really angry and didn't speak for the rest of the evening. Afterwards, I discovered why: . . . !

H Vocabulary practice. Complete these sentences, using the words in the box.

| bargain | clothes | hole | secondhand | town centre |
| care for | familiar | mend | smart | wardrobe |

1 If you buy any more . . . , you'll need to get a bigger . . . !
2 I got this jacket . . . . It was an absolute . . . !
3 Your suitcase has got a . . . in it. Why don't you try to . . . it?
4 Everything looked different. I recognised the . . . , but nothing else was . . . .
5 Do you really think those jeans are . . . ? To be honest, I don't . . . them at all.

I Discussion

Do you keep clothes that you do not wear very often? (Why?) Most people have a favourite piece of clothing – a shirt or a pair of jeans. What is yours?

Section 2 Cloze practice

1 Put in *a, an* or *the*.

... two boys cleaned out ... hut and lit ... fire. Then they had supper. They were both tired and they did not talk much. Before they went to bed, they put plenty of wood on ... fire. George fell asleep almost at once, but Fred lay awake for ... long time, watching ... flames. Then he too fell asleep.

Suddenly he was awake again. ... fire was nearly out. He could hear noises outside. It sounded like voices. He woke up George. "It's only ... wind," he grumbled. "Go to sleep again!"

But it wasn't ... wind! ... voices came nearer until they were just outside ... hut. ... door opened and ... light shone on their faces. "They're here!" ... voice called out. ... policeman was standing in ... doorway. He addressed ... two boys. "You've given us ... lot of trouble," he said. "We've looked all over ... valley for you two!"

2 Put in the verb forms.

We were ... on the bridge, trying to ... some fish for supper when a small red plane ... almost directly above our heads. We could even ... the pilot's face. "What on earth ... he up to?" I ... . I ... rather annoyed.

"I ... he's in trouble," Jack ... . "His engine is ... a strange noise."

"Well, we can't ... anything, can we?" I ... . "We ... even phone from here." We ... on a boating holiday and we ... miles from the nearest town.

"We can ... the plane down the river," Jack ... . "... on! Let's ... !"

3 Put in the prepositions.

... the top ... the stairs Alan made old Mr Cox climb ... his back. Then he put a handkerchief ... his own face and went ... the stairs as quickly as he could. There was a cheer ... the crowd as he came ... ... the house.

The fire engine and an ambulance arrived more or less ... that moment. The first flames were just beginning to come ... ... the front window. "It's all my fault," moaned old Mr Cox as they carried him ... the ambulance. "I was reading the newspaper and I left it ... the electric fire."

4 Put in the missing words.

We had an enormous apple tree in our ... only a few yards from the kitchen window.

"We really must ... that tree down," my husband said, soon after we moved into the ... . "I'm sure it's ... ."

"... be silly," I said. I quite liked the ... myself. "It's quite safe. It isn't going to ... down on the house!"

"Well, I read something in the ... only the other day," he said. "A tree crashed into a woman's bedroom during a ... . She was going to get ... of the tree – and now she's in ... !"

In the end, after several ... of this kind, we asked a couple of ... to come along and cut the tree down. It was not an easy . . . . In fact, it took them . . . morning. But at last the tree was lying on the . . . .

5 Put in the verb forms.

Lacey . . . the yard. He . . . the window without difficulty and . . . through. But the kitchen door . . . locked and the key . . . not there. He . . . to the window and . . . to Barnes.

"You'll have to . . . through the window, too," he . . . .

Just at that moment they . . . the sound of a car. It was . . . the house at great speed and its lights . . . up the house as it . . . nearer. People . . . out and they could . . . voices.

"It's the police," Barnes . . . . "It's a trap. I . . . it!"

"Don't . . . !" Lacey . . . him. "Now . . . to me. . . . back to the car and . . . for me there. I'll . . . you as soon as I can. Off you . . . – and . . . well in the shadows."

6 Put in the pronouns.

Oct 26 . . . tried to explain some of my problems to my supervisor today. . . . listened – but that was about all. ". . . have to go to lectures, . . . know, Ann," . . . told . . . . "And the hostel *is* cheap and convenient." 'Cheap and convenient!' Well, . . . isn't 'cheap' if . . . can't eat the food and . . . isn't 'convenient' if . . . can't sleep at night!

Oct 30 . . . can't believe . . . ! Three other students – . . . met . . . at a lecture and . . . 're all about my own age – have invited . . . to share a flat with . . . . 's in an old house and . . . has its own kitchen, so . . . can cook for ourselves.

7 Put in *a*, *an* or *the*.

. . . few years ago, while I was on holiday in . . . Himalayas, I stopped for . . . night in . . . small village. It was . . . very poor place and there was no proper hotel, but . . . owner of . . . restaurant offered me . . . bed for . . . night.

"Please wait here," he said, pointing to . . . table just outside his restaurant, "while I prepare your room."

It was . . . beautiful evening. . . . sun was setting behind . . . dark mountains and . . . stars were just beginning to come out. . . . villagers were lighting fires for their evening meals and there was . . . pleasant smell of wood smoke in . . . air.

Then I noticed that I was no longer alone. Someone was sitting at . . . table beside me. It was . . . old man with . . . long white beard.

8 Put in the prepositions.

"Maybe," Roy replied. "But the trouble is, I always dream . . . hard work! Last night, . . . example, I dreamt I was a miner. I went . . . the mine almost as soon as I fell asleep – and I dreamt that I was digging coal all night long. I was worn out . . . the morning! Then, a few nights ago, I dreamt I was a sailor. I was . . . one . . . those old fashioned sailing ships. We were crossing the Atlantic and there was a terrific storm. We had to struggle... hours to stop the ship... going down. It's always like that. ... the past few weeks, I've dreamt I was a waiter, a lorry driver and a football player. I never have a nice easy job!"

"I was reading an article... sleep... a magazine the other day," his brother said. "The writer's advice was: try to relax before you go... sleep."

9 Put in the verb forms.

"I... it wandering through the park," Jane.... "It... so lonely! I... to it and we... friends at once. And then it... me back here."

"Well, you... you can't... it," her mother.... "You'd better... the police and...."

Not long after, the police... and also a van from the zoo. Nobody... even angry with Jane when she... her story. The police... all about Jane and her animals. And the zoo keeper...: "I can... that Gor... you. But we... him back at the zoo! But you can... and... him as often as you.... We'll... you a free pass!"

10 Put in the missing words.

They drifted on and... through the clouds. Every moment Andy expected the balloon to... the side of the mountain. But it... happened. Suddenly... were out in the sunlight again. "The... is," Pete said, "I'm not... exactly where we are now!" Andy looked.... "Isn't that a farm down...?" he asked, pointing to some buildings. "... don't we land and ask?" Peter hesitated. They were lost, but he did not... to ask for help.

"All...," he said in the end.

A few... later, they made a perfect landing only a couple of hundred... from the farmhouse.

11 Put in the prepositions.

Robert was a good swimmer and he hesitated... only a moment. Taking... his coat, he dived... the river. The icy water almost took his breath..., but... a matter... seconds he reached the boy. "Don't panic!" he said as he caught hold... him. "Just relax – and I'll soon get you... ... the water.'

But the boy began to struggle and shout something... him. Robert could not make... his words. "Don't panic," he said again and started... swim... the bank, dragging the boy... him. But... that moment he noticed a large motor boat... the bridge. There were several people... board, all looking... his direction. Robert decided... swim... the boat.

12 Put in the verb forms.

I always... the drive into Marley. It... a good straight road, with some pleasant views of the countryside on either side. There... woods and hills, villages and farms and, about halfway, a large lake. And because there... rarely much traffic on the road, I can usually... the view as I... along.

I...rather annoyed the other morning, therefore, when a small green car began to...very close behind me. I...a little faster, hoping to...the car behind. But whenever I...down, the little car...up with me. The driver, a middle-aged man, was...and...to me. However, I did not...either him or the car.

13 Put in the missing words.
Johnny continued to 'see places' although everyone tried to...him. His parents used to...him closely, and so...his teachers; but sooner or...Johnny managed to slip away. As he...older, his favourite trick was to hide on a long distance.... Sometimes he used to travel hundreds of...before anyone discovered him. It is...surprising that eventually Johnny managed to get on board a.... He was twelve at the time. It was a cargo plane, and, a few...later, Johnny found himself in Cairo. How did he get on...? No one...! According to Johnny himself, it was...: he just went into the..., walked along some corridors and got on board the...plane.

14 Put in the pronouns.
"A holiday abroad? Yes, of course, Mrs Green. ...'m sure...can arrange something for..."

The travel agent smiled at the old lady across the counter. ...knew...well. At one time, years before,...and her husband used to go to Brighton every summer. In those days,...booked a family hotel for.... Then...started to take their holidays in France – and...got...their boat tickets. Later, when their children grew up,...'discovered' Italy and Spain. ...bought their air tickets or found cheap holidays for....

But then, the previous autumn, Mr Green died. "Well, no more holidays abroad for Mrs Green,"...thought. "...'ll probably start going to Brighton again!"

But...was wrong! Here...was, only a few months after her husband's death, back in his office asking about holidays abroad.

15 Put in a, an or the.
Later I went along to...Job Centre. I filled in...form and had...interview with...clerk. She was quite pleasant, really, but she asked me...lot of silly questions! Anyway, she hadn't got...job to offer me. I have to go back there on Wednesday.

Tuesday I called in at...bank today and checked my account. At least I'm not short of money – for...moment. Then I walked past...office where I used to work. Through...windows I could see people working inside. I felt envious! Afterwards, I sat in...cafe, thinking. If there's nothing at...Job Centre tomorrow, I'll ring my old friend Liz. She usually has some ideas.

16 Put in the missing words.
"What's all the mystery?" I.... "Tell me all...it!"

"It isn't exactly a..., Kay" Nicky began. I waited for her to...on. "Well, do you remember that woman who used to ... opposite the church — Miss Hunter?"

"The one who used to wear funny ... and had a large dog? Wasn't ... an artist?"

"Well, ... ," Nicky said. "She did paint — ... only as a hobby. As a matter of ... , she was a writer — and I've just bought her latest ... !" Nicky ... the book out of her bag and passed ... across the table. The ... was 'Death Comes to the Village'.

17 Put in the verb forms.

When a cheque for £200,000 ... in the post one morning, Mrs Wood nearly ... . She ... the football pools every week, but she never ... to win anything. She never ... it to her family because she did not ... them to ... at her. Her husband and her son Ron ... all about football. They ... the pools every week too and quite often ... a few pounds.

The family ... in the kitchen when she ... in ... the cheque, unable to ... a word. Her husband ... the cheque from her and ... it in the middle of the kitchen table. Her son made her ... down and her daughter Diane ... her a cup of tea. Two hundred thousand pounds! They ... all about Mrs Wood and began to ... about the money.

18 Put in the prepositions.

We left ... time (and ... plenty ... loud music!) and stopped ... supper ... a cafe ... about 9.30. It wasn't the sort ... place I like eating ... and it was also very crowded, so I decided ... buy some chocolate. I had some fruit ... me too, so ... least I didn't go hungry.

We set ... again ... 10.15. The lights went ... (and the awful music too, thank goodness) and I settled ... to get some sleep. However, the people just ... me kept ... talking and every now and then they burst ... laughing ... some joke. I asked them ... be quiet, but they didn't take any notice ... all. However, eventually I fell asleep — but then the people ... me woke me ... ! "You're snoring," they said, "and keeping us awake!" ... that I hardly slept ... all.

19 Put in *a, an* or *the*.

One summer evening, just as he was getting ready to go to bed, Rod heard ... low humming noise outside, like thousands of bees. He looked out of his bedroom window. In ... field at ... end of ... garden he saw ... number of bright objects coming down. As they landed, their lights went out and ... field became dark. Rod decided to take ... closer look from ... wall at ... end of his garden.

From there he could see ... mysterious objects quite clearly. There were twelve of them in all and they were long and thin, like enormous cigars. In ... centre of ... machines he could just make out ... group of figures, all wearing space suits. They appeared to be having ... meeting.

20 Put in the verb forms.

Nick... bored with life. Every day... exactly the same. He... up at exactly the same time; he... the same bus to work; he... the same things in the office; he... to the same people; he... home at the same time; he... the same programmes on television – and he... to bed at the same time!

"What I... is a little adventure!" Nick... as he... at the bus stop one morning. Nick's 'little adventure'... sooner than he...!

While he... on the bus,... his newspaper (the same one that he... every morning), the man... next to him suddenly... a large brown envelope into his hands. "Here,... this!" he.... Then he... up and... off the bus before Nick could... a word.

21 Put in the missing words.

It was my birthday... Thursday and I decided to celebrate it by... a few friends out to supper. I chose a restaurant in a quiet... of town. It is one of my favourite restaurants... the food is good and the... are friendly. It is hardly... crowded, however, because few people... about it, so it is not usually necessary to... a table. In any case, Thursday is not a... evening as a rule.

When we... the restaurant, I was surprised, therefore, to find it completely.... I looked around – but not a single... was free. One of the waiters... me. He came across and... the situation. "A... of tourists came in about half an hour ago," he said. "It was... an invasion! Suddenly the... was full! We... hardly manage!"

22 Put in the pronouns.

Thank... for your letter. ... 'm sorry to hear... 're having problems with the flat. ... can't solve... all, of course, but... 'll try to be helpful.

1 *Furniture*... liked... when... moved in! ... told... so! But now... 've changed your mind. Well,... 'm sorry... can't help... there.

2 *Heating*... agree that the flat can be cold in winter. ... lived there myself for twenty years, so... know! But... always used electric fires and... 'm afraid... must do the same. But get someone to look at the windows, by all means.

3 *Kitchen* Yes,... probably does need painting. Your idea is a good one. Please buy the paint and send... the bill.

23 Put in the prepositions.

The interviewer led me... a small room next... the studio and gestured... an armchair. "Take a seat," he said. "I've sent... some coffee. It'll be here... a moment."

He was a tall young man, thin,... dark glasses and longish hair. He wore old jeans and an Indian style shirt.

"Right," he said, sitting... opposite me and opening a notebook. "Let me tell you something... the programme. I'll begin... introducing you – and saying a few nice words...you! Then we'll start talking. Most...the time I'll ask questions, but if you like, you can just keep...talking. OK?"

"OK!" I said.

"Well now, let's see. I need to check a few facts...you. You were born...Dublin – when was it? – thirty seven years ago. You went...university...England – ...London. But you didn't take a degree, I see. Why was that?"

"Oh, I got bored," I explained. "I didn't like spending all my time...libraries and lecture rooms."

24 Put in a, an or the.

All...time, of course, she was looking for...small part in...film. Her big chance came when they started to make...film in our town. Jane managed to meet...director at...party, and he offered her...role as...shopkeeper. It really was...very small part – she only had...few lines to say – but it was...important moment for Jane. Before...great event, she rehearsed for days. In fact, she turned...sitting-room into...shop! We all had to help, going in and out of...shop until she was word perfect. And on...actual day she was marvellous. ...director congratulated her. Jane thought that this was...beginning of her film career!

25 Put in the verb forms.

Everything...well for the first ten miles. Then I...to a steep hill. Well, I managed to...the top without...off my bike (much to my surprise!) and...to go downhill. And then the trouble...! The brakes didn't...! I...them again and again, but it...no use. I...really scared, I can...you! I...on trying the brakes – and suddenly they did...! Of course by this time I was...much too fast and I...off the bike into some bushes. I...my left arm,...my shoulder and I...cuts and bruises all over. I...lucky I didn't...my neck!

26 Put in the missing words.

Andy Barton was in a...mood. It was Friday, and at six o'clock his favourite..., *Travel with us*, was on TV. Andy liked to...home in good time for that. But then, just as he was...the office a little early, a customer rang up with a...complaints. The customer...steadily for the next fifteen minutes!

"I can still get home in...if I hurry," Andy told himself as he dashed out of the.... But then, as he drove off in his..., he noticed that he was almost out of.... "I'll have to stop at Fenton's," Andy.... He...Fenton's because it was a self-service petrol station. "You do all the...yourself, but you pay the...for the petrol," he used to grumble.

27 Put in the prepositions.

The phone rang...Dr Allen's desk.

"Hello," she said, picking...the phone. "Dr Allen here."

"Oh, good morning, Dr Allen," a voice said. "It's Jenny Anderson here,

Professor Smith's secretary. It's... that meeting... Monday. You are definitely coming, aren't you?"

"The meeting. Yes,... course," Dr Allen said, looking... her diary. "It's... eleven, I see."

"Well, no. We had... change the time," Jenny Anderson said. "It's going to be... twelve. I'm sure I told you."

"But I've got a lecture... twelve," Dr Allen said.

"But surely you can cancel your lecture – just... once," Jenny Anderson suggested. "The meeting's very important, as you know."

"I've never cancelled a lecture... my life," Dr Allen told her. "Sorry!"

28 Put in the verb forms.

Then a bell... and within seconds the corridor... full of noisy boys, all... and .... They... like a great flood, almost... Tandem along with them. He... glad when he finally... the door of the headmaster's study.

He... at the door and.... "... in!" a voice... out. The headmaster... up to... him as he... in. He... an old man now and Tandem hardly... him.

"Good afternoon, Tandem," the headmaster.... "So you... an inspector now! Well, quite a few boys... back to... their old school, but no one has ever... back to... it before!"

29 Put in the pronouns.

... looked under my own papers, and then on the floor, but there was no sign of my watch. ... was not in my pockets, either.

"... didn't put... in your bag, did...?" ... asked Mark. "Along with your papers." ... checked, but the watch was not there.

"...'s very odd," ... said. "... remember taking... off and putting... on the table when... started work. No one's been near... except the ticket collector – and... didn't pick... up!"

"Someone came and cleared away the coffee cups," Mark said. "... remember seeing a man with a big plastic bag."

The man with the plastic bag came from the restaurant car, one of the passengers informed.... ... went along there to see... and... explained my problem.

30 Put in the missing words.

I divided my clothes into... piles: those I wore..., those I... ever wore and, finally, those I... wore at all. I decided to get rid of... the things in the second and third... and I put them into a....

But I couldn't make up my... about one thing: an old grey jacket. I hardly ever... it, but I liked it. It fitted me...! and it looked smart. But it was old, and there was a... near one of the pockets. I tried to... it, but the cotton I used was the wrong.... So, in the end, I put the... into the suitcase along with the other clothes and set off to find a secondhand clothes.... I found... near the town centre.

103

Section 3 Vocabulary activities

1

A Give the past tense forms of these verbs. (Note: you can find them in the text)

come; fall (asleep); go; lie (awake); light; put; run; say; shine; sit; wake up.

B Put in the prepositions: *at, for, in*.

... the most; ... a while; ... the doorway.

C Divide these words into opposite pairs. e.g. day – night.

day; downhill; inside; large; night; nothing; outside; run; sit down; small; something; stand up; uphill; walk.

2

A Give the past tense forms of these verbs.

can; feel; fly; know.

B Put in the prepositions: *at, in, in, on, of, of*.

... trouble; ... once; ... front ... us; ... top ... the plane.

C Which word is different? e.g. in 1, pilot is different.

1 lake; pilot; river; water.
2 annoyed; bored; damp; exhausted.
3 dropped; raced; ran; walked.

3

A Give the past tense forms of these verbs.

begin; leave; make; put; tell.

B What are the opposites of these words?

asleep; back; downstairs; outside.

C Which words in the text are connected with 'house'?

e.g. window

4

A Give the past tense forms of these verbs.

find; hide; read; take.

B Put in the prepositions: *at, in, in, on*.

... the paper; ... hospital; ... last; ... the ground.

104

C What adjectives in the text are used to describe these words?
coins; hole; job; rubbish; tree.

5

A Give the past tense forms of these verbs.
creep; get; hear; see.

B Which of these words are plural?
clothes; edge; gloves; key; men; people; police; voices; yard.

C Which word is different?
1 dog; gun; key; tool.
2 climb; creep; cross; sit.
3 men; police; people; shadows.

Consolidation

A Find pairs of related words, taking a word from each box.
e.g. ambulance – hospital.

ambulance	plane	storm
fire	ring	tree
house	river	workman

engine	kitchen	roots
fish	jewellery	smoke
hospital	job	wind

B Give more examples.

clothes	*house*	*jewellery*	*people*	*places*	*transport*
gloves	kitchen	rings	firemen	lake	boat

C Which word is different?
1 ask; say; tell; whistle.
2 fire; flames; signal; smoke.
3 fireman; husband; pilot; policeman.
4 hospital; house; hut; street.
5 hill; river; trap; valley.

6

A Which words in the text are used to describe these?
hostel food; hostel building; lectures; main road; room in hostel; room in flat; students.

B Give examples of:
buildings (e.g. hostel); rooms (e.g. kitchen); food (e.g. bread).

C Put in the prepositions: *at, of, from*.

. . . course; . . . night; . . . now on.

7

A Give the past tense forms of these verbs.

begin; hold; take; think.

B Make the -ing form of each of these verbs. e.g. sit – sitting, come – coming.

begin; believe; describe; get; live; set; smile; stop.

C Which word is different?

1 behind; beside; prepare; without.
2 dirty; firmly; gently; softly.

8

A 'Miner' is a job. Find 7 more jobs in the text.

B Make a noun from each of these verbs. e.g. play – player (= someone who plays).

listen; own; read; speak; wait; work.

C Divide these words into opposite pairs. e.g. badly – well.

badly; day; different; easy; future; hard; night; noisy; past; quiet; same; well.

9

A Give the past tense forms of these verbs.

bring; catch; have; make; stand.

B Which word is different?

1 bedroom; garden; park; zoo.
2 house; hut; shed; van.

C Find examples in the text of:

animals; food.

10

A Who or what was . . . ?

busy; fine; hot; interesting; nervous; perfect; thick; wonderful.

B Put in the prepositions: *by, from, in, out of*.

. . . . . . sight; . . . the sunlight; a long way . . . home; . . . balloon.

C Which word is different?
1 companion; farms; rivers; villages.
2 through; towards; wind; within.

Consolidation
A Find pairs of related words, taking a word from each box.
e.g. crowd – people.

crowd	mine	ship
hostel	orchestra	sky
library	park	zoo

animals	coal	sailors
books	people	students
clouds	players	trees

B Find pairs of similar words. e.g. hills – mountains.
begin; close to; disappear; enormous; exhausted; hills; huge; mountains; near; pictures; posters; start; tired; vanish.

C Divide these words into opposite pairs. e.g. asleep – awake.
asleep; awake; back; beautiful; breakfast; dangerous; downstairs; front; future; inside; large; noisy; outside; past; quiet; safe; small; supper; ugly; upstairs.

D Which word is different?
1 ambulance; lorry; plane; van.
2 bridge; path; road; street.
3 afternoon; evening; midnight; morning.
4 concrete; metal; water; wood.

11
A Make a noun from each of these verbs. e.g. walk – walker, swim – swimmer.
begin; climb; dream; lecture; run; smoke; speak.

B Put in the prepositions: *in, in, of, on.*
. . . the water; . . . a matter . . . seconds; . . . board.

C Which of these words are connected with 'river'?
bank; blanket; boats; bridge; canoe; dived; float; hand; jacket; row; swimmer; water.

12
A Give the past tense forms of these verbs.
catch; drive; fall.

B Which word is different?
1 indicator; lights; miles; number plate.
2 field; lake; traffic; wood.
3 drive; go; grin; slow down.

C Give examples of things you can find in 'traffic'.
e.g. cars, lorries, . . .

13

A The following words can be used as nouns or verbs. How are they used in the text?
address; answer; board; cross; garden; name; notice; question; trick; walk; work.

B Notice: unhappy = not happy. Now make more adjectives with un-.
fortunate; helpful; interesting; pleasant; safe; true.

C Put in the prepositions: for, in, of, on, on, to.
. . . the first time; . . . foot; . . . spite . . . all this; . . . his way . . . Brazil.

14

A Give the past tense forms of these verbs.
buy; find; grow; shake.

B Are these words used as verbs or nouns in the text?
book; guide; smile; surprise; tour.

C Which word is different?
1 autumn; summer; winter; year.
2 book; brochure; newspaper; ticket.
3 age; mouth; week; year.

15

A Give the past tense forms of these verbs.
lose; ring; see; sit.

B Put in the prepositions: for, for, of, on.
. . . once; . . . a while; . . . Wednesday; short . . . money.

C Which word is different?
1 bank; cafe; hotel; restaurant.
2 clerk; dreamer; teacher; travel agent.
3 camera; computer; office; television.

Consolidation

A Link nouns and verbs. e.g. attract – attention.

answer	check	fill in
attract	dive	make
book	drive	wear

account	film	jacket
attention	form	question
car	hotel	water

B Find pairs of related words, taking a word from each box.
e.g. airport – plane.

airport	car	road
bank	office	school
bed	restaurant	train

account	food	teacher
blanket	plane	ticket
clerk	puncture	traffic

C Find pairs of similar words. e.g. annoyed – cross.

annoyed; cross; difficult; fast; happy; hard; hesitate; pause; phone; pleased; quickly; ring up.

D Which word is different?

1 brochure; magazine; newspaper; ticket.
2 today; tomorrow; year; yesterday.
3 December; Friday; November; October.
4 run; swim; walk; wander.
5 breath; eye; foot; head.
6 cross; glad; happy; pleased.
7 expedition; tour; trick; trip.

16

A Divide these words into two groups: shops and people.

artist; baker; baker's; bookshop; chemist; chemist's; detective; greengrocer; greengrocer's; postwoman; supermarket; writer.

B Put in the prepositions: *in, of, of, with*.

... a quarter ... an hour; as a matter ... fact; pleased ... herself.

C Which word is different?

1 bag; book; magazine; newspaper.
2 artist; hobby; postwoman; writer.
3 bookshop; cafe; church; clothes.

17

A Give the past tenses of these verbs.

begin; break out; forget; win.

B Which word is different?

1 account; bank; cheque; diary.
2 daughter; friend; husband; son.
3 computer; poster; television; video.
4 nice; selfish; stupid; unpleasant.

C Which of these words are connected with 'money'?

argument; business; buy; charity; cheque; football pools; pocket; post; profits; pounds.

18

A Form verbs, taking a word from each box. e.g. set off.

break	keep	set
burst	long	settle
go	send	

down	for	on
down	off	out
for	off	

B Put in the prepositions: *for, in, in, on*.

... time; ... the rain; ... the end; thanks ... the advice.

C Which word is different?

1 bread; chocolate; fruit; stone.
2 exhausted; hungry; tired; worn out.

19

A Give the past tense forms of these verbs.

become; fall; rise; stand.

B Which word is different?

1 depressed; glad; sad; unhappy.
2 field; garden; wall; yard.
3 cigar; indicator; number plate; wheel.

C Divide these words into opposite pairs. e.g. high – low.

asleep; awake; day; fat; high; land; long; loud; low; night; quiet; short; summer; take off; thin; winter.

20

A Form verbs, taking a word from each box. e.g. get off.

get	hand	wait
go	make	

for	on	up
off	over	

B Put in the prepositions: *in, in, on, with*.
bored . . . life; . . . television; no longer . . . sight; . . . all the newspapers.

C Find pairs of similar words. e.g. big – large.
afraid; big; clearly; close to; fast; give; hand over; invent; large; make up; near; obviously; quickly; sorry.

Consolidation

A Make nouns, taking a word from each box. e.g. air ticket.

air	job	rescue
bus	lorry	traffic
football	police	travel

agent	lights	stop
centre	pools	ticket
driver	station	van

B Find pairs of related words, taking a word from each box. e.g. baker's – bread.

baker's	magazine
bank	postman
greengrocer's	shopping
Job Centre	travel agent

article	holiday
bread	letters
cheques	list
fruit	unemployment

C Make *-er* type nouns. e.g. teacher, runner etc.
advise; begin; dream; garden; interview; rescue; shop; talk; travel; win.

D Which word is different?
1 envelope; letter; machine; postman.
2 clerk; office; papers; wheel.
3 bee; flying saucer; outer space; planet.
4 driver; field; garage; van.
5 crowd; gang; group; object.

21

A Make adjectives with *un-*.

comfortable; fortunate; friendly; happy; necessary.

B Link verb and noun, taking a word from each box. e.g. attract – attention.

attract	order
book	
celebrate	pay

attention	food
bill	table
birthday	

C Which words in the text are connected with 'restaurant'? e.g. food.

22

A Put in the prepositions: *at, by, in, in, in*.

... bad condition; ... winter; ... any case; ... all means; ... the same time.

B Which word is different?

1 armchair; bed; table; window.
2 bathroom; garden; kitchen; sitting room.
3 flat; hotel; house; shed.

C Divide these words into opposite pairs. e.g. a long way off – near.

a long way off; buy; cheap; empty; expensive; full; glad; near; sell; sorry; summer; winter

23

A Link verb and noun, taking a word from each box. e.g. catch fire.

| catch | read | spend |
| pass | shake | take |

| book | fire | time |
| degree | head | time |

B Which word is different?

1 coat; handkerchief; jeans; shirt.
2 passenger; ship; steward; studio.
3 tour; trip; view; voyage.
4 degree; lecture; supper; university.
5 diary; form; newspaper; notebook.

C **Which words in the text are connected with 'ship'?** e.g. steward.

24

A **Put in the prepositions: *at, at, for, in, of, on, over*.**

well . . . seventy; . . . least; . . . television; . . . one thing; . . . dozens . . . films; . . . a party.

B **Form verbs, taking a word from each box.** e.g. close down.

close	give	turn
cut	look	

down	into	up
for	out	

C **Which word is different?**
1 actress; director; immigrant; shopkeeper.
2 blow; lines; part; role.
3 enjoy; like; love; rehearse.

25

A **Put in the prepositions: *by, by, in, of, on, on*.**

. . . holiday; . . . the end . . . the week; . . . car; . . . a few days; . . . my way home.

B **Are these words used as verbs or nouns in the text?**

cut; promise; rest; sleep; surprise; trouble; use; walk; work.

C **Which word is different?**
1 arm; neck; place; shoulder.
2 bike; boat; car; van.
3 friendly; nice; pleasant; terrible.

Consolidation

A **Give the past tense forms of these verbs. Note: the number of the text is given in brackets.**

break (25); choose (21); eat (25); lead (21); lend (25); meet (25); send (21); set off (25); shake (23); take (25); tell (22); think (25); wear (23); write (23).

B **Make nouns, taking a word from each box.** e.g. crowd scene.

crowd	lecture	rest
film	railway	sitting

period	room	station
room	scene	studio

C Divide these words into opposite pairs. e.g. beginning – end.

beginning; boring; bottom; breakfast; comic; early; empty; end; fast; finish; full; interesting; late; old; serious; short; slowly; start; supper; tall; top; young.

D Which word is different?

1 shopkeeper; steward; tourist; waiter.
2 camera; film; office; studio.
3 enormous; full; huge; large.
4 bill; degree; restaurant; waiter.
5 holiday; invasion; tourist; travel agent.
6 aunt; mother; sister; parent.

26

A Put in the prepositions: *in, in, in, on, out of, to.*

... a bad mood; ... good time; ... ... petrol; ... his way ... Japan; ... the same street.

B Which word is different?

1 Friday; May; Sunday; Wednesday.
2 garage; petrol; police; pump.
3 Australia; India; Japan; Montreal.

C Divide these words into opposite pairs. e.g. arrive – leave.

arrive; close; different; forget; glad; hate; keep on; leave; love; open; same; stop; sorry; remember.

27

A Form verbs, taking a word from each box. e.g. listen to.

B Put in the prepositions: *at, for, in, in, to.*

just ... once; ... fact; ... two places ... once; ... her surprise.

C Which word is different?

1 chair; counter; desk; table.
2 conference; meeting; party; programme.
3 cassette recorder; notebook; radio; television.

28

A **Divide these words into two groups, *subjects* and *rooms*.**

biology; chemistry; classroom; geography; laboratory; library; maths; physics; staffroom; study.

B **Put in the prepositions: *for, on, on, round*.**

. . . a moment; . . . the left; . . . the first floor; a quick look . . . the school.

C **Which word is different?**

1 noisy; peaceful; pleasant; quiet.
2 helpful; nervous; scared; worried.
3 headmaster; secretary; student; teacher.

29

A **Form verbs, taking a word from each box.** e.g. clear away.

clear	pick	settle
empty	put	take
hold		

away	off	out
away	on	up
down		

B **Make nouns, taking a word from each box.** e.g. coffee cup.

coffee	plastic	ticket
corner	restaurant	

bag	cup	seat
car	inspector	

C **Which word is different?**

1 concrete; meat; metal; plastic.
2 biscuits; bread; flowers; fruit.
3 journey; meeting; trip; voyage.

30

A **Form verbs, taking a word from each box.** e.g. care for.

care	make	set
get rid	pick	turn

for	off	up
of	over	up

B   Which word is different?

1   glasses; shirt; suit; trousers.
2   bag; box; pocket; suitcase.
3   armchair; door; table; wardrobe.

C   Divide these words into opposite pairs. e.g. always – never.

always; brother; badly; buy; hate; love; never; new; secondhand; sell; sister; well.

Consolidation

A   What are the past tense forms of these verbs?

begin; break out; bring; buy; catch; choose; drive; fall; find; fly; grow; hide; hold; know; leave; lie; lose; meet; rise; run; see; shake; sit; stand; take; think; wake; wear; win; write.

B   Divide these verbs into two groups, those like *say* (e.g. admit, answer) and those like *go* (e.g. approach, come).

admit; answer; approach; ask; call; come; cry; dash; enter; exclaim; explain; follow; grumble; hurry; inform; lead; leave; mutter; reply; run; rush; shout; snap; travel; walk; wander.

C   Divide these words into similar pairs. e.g. answer – reply.

answer; children; clearly; dash; disappear; examine; excuse; fortunately; give; hand over; inspect; kids; journey; luckily; obviously; odd; one; peaceful; quiet; reason; reply; rush; single; steward; strange; trip; vanish; waiter.

D   How many can you remember?

1   Animals: rabbit, . . .
2   Buildings: hotel, . . .
3   Clothes: coat, . . .
4   Countryside: lake, . . .
5   Days: Monday, . . .
6   Food: bread, . . .
7   Furniture: table, . . .
8   Jobs: waiter, . . .
9   Months: March, . . .
10 Relationships: husband, . . .
11 Rooms: sitting room, . . .
12 Shops: greengrocer's, . . .
13 Seasons: spring, . . .
14 Subjects: geography, . . .
15 Transport: car, . . .

Section 4 Dictation passages

1

The hut was among some trees / on the side of the valley. / It was damp inside, / but we cleaned it out / and lit a fire. / There was plenty of wood / in the hut. / Then we had supper. / We were both exhausted / and we did not talk much. / George fell asleep / almost at once. / I lay awake, / watching the flames. / Then I fell asleep too. / Suddenly I heard a noise outside. / I woke up George. / What was it? / Was it voices / or only the wind? / The door opened. / A light shone on our faces. / It was a policeman.

(After CP 1)

2

We saw the smoke / from the end of the street. / The smoke was coming / out of the window / of our front room. / There was a small crowd / outside the house, / but there was no sign / of Elsa's old father. / Elsa's father / lived with us. / He had a room upstairs / at the back of the house. / When we went out, / he was sitting in the front room, / reading a newspaper / near the electric fire. / I ran into the house / and raced up the stairs. / Elsa's father / was in his room, / sleeping peacefully.

(After CP 3)

3

The two men / crept round the edge of the garden / and went across the yard / towards the back of the big house. / They opened the kitchen window / without difficulty, / and climbed through. / In one of the bedrooms / they found a small metal box. / They broke the box open. / It was full of jewellery: / rings, / necklaces / and bracelets. / But just at that moment / they heard the sound / of a police car. / It was approaching the house / at great speed. / Its lights / lit up the house / and policemen got out. / It was a trap!

(After CP 5)

4

There was a restaurant / near the main road / and we sometimes went there for supper / because the food in the hostel / was awful. / The owner of the restaurant / liked to tell fortunes. / One evening / he told me about my childhood, / and every word was true. / He wanted to tell me / about the future too, / but it was already very late. / Not long after that / I moved into a flat / with three other students. / We had our own kitchen, / so we were able to cook / for ourselves. / I never went back / to the restaurant, / so I never heard / about my future!

(After CP 7)

117

5

I dream a lot. / Doctors say / that dreaming is good for you, / but the trouble is / I dream about hard work! / When I wake up / the next morning, / I always feel tired. / I asked my brother / for some advice. / He told me to relax / before going to sleep. / He gave me a magazine / with an article about animals. / It was full of pictures. / That night / I dreamt I was in a zoo. / The animals escaped / and followed me home. / They stayed in the garden / and made a lot of noise. / I couldn't sleep at all! / The next morning, / when I woke up, / I was more tired / than usual.

(After CP 9)

6

It was a cold afternoon. / Pete was standing on the bridge, / watching a big balloon. / The balloon was coming down / very slowly, / but it was going / straight into the river. / Every moment / Pete expected it / to hit the water. / But it never happened. / It made a perfect landing / on the bank of the river. / However, / the two men in the balloon / began to struggle / and shout. / Perhaps they needed help. / Pete started to run / towards the balloon. / But just at that moment / a motorboat appeared / from under the bridge. / The people on the boat / had large cameras. / They were making a film!

(After CP 11)

7

The other day / while I was driving into town, / I had to slow down / because there was a lorry / just in front of me. / I was surprised to see / a boy of about ten / on the back of the lorry. / He even waved / and grinned at me. / What was the boy / doing there? / Perhaps he was running / away from home. / I decided to say something / to the driver of the lorry. / The lorry had to stop / at some traffic lights / so I got out / and spoke to the driver. / I was right. / The boy / was running away from home. / He often did this / and sometimes / covered hundreds of miles / before anyone discovered him.

(After CP 13)

8

Something awful / happened the other day. / I lost my job. / At first / I felt very depressed. / But I checked my bank account: / for the moment at least / I am not short of money. / I spend a lot of time / in the library / reading guidebooks, / because I have plans / to travel. / Yesterday / I was reading a book about India. It said / that hotels and food / are very cheap there. / You can also travel everywhere / by bus or train. / Perhaps I can go to India / for a long holiday. / All

I need / is a cheap air ticket. / Tomorrow / I have definitely decided / to go to a travel agent.

(After CP 15)

9

For years Mrs Wood / worked for Miss Hunter, / who lived opposite the church. / Miss Hunter / wrote detective stories. / She often said / that one day / she was going to write a book / about Mrs Wood. / Mrs Wood used to laugh. / She was not a great reader, / except for newspapers / and magazines. / Then one day / Miss Hunter died / and Mrs Wood lost her job. / She felt very depressed / until one morning / someone rang her up. / Mrs Wood had to go / to his office. / "You're a rich woman!" / the man told her. / "Miss Hunter has left you / two hundred thousand pounds!" / Mrs Wood nearly fainted.

(After CP 17)

10

One evening last summer / Rod had a strange experience / while he was travelling / by coach. / The coach stopped for supper / at a cafe. / Rod was not hungry, / so he stayed in the coach. / As he sat there, / eating some chocolate, / he saw a number of objects / landing in a field / not far from the cafe. / Rod rushed out of the coach / and ran / towards the mysterious objects. / There were twelve of them / in all. / Rod felt sure / that they were flying saucers. / At that moment, / however, / the strange machines / started to leave / and a wave of hot air / pushed Rod to the ground. / When he opened his eyes, / the field was empty.

(After CP 19)

11

It was my birthday / last Friday, / so I invited some friends / to have supper with me / in one of my favourite restaurants. / It was completely full / when we went in, / so we had to wait / for a table. / Luckily, / after about ten minutes, / a party of tourists / at a corner table / got up and left. / As we sat down / at their table, / I noticed a large brown envelope / on one of the chairs. / I picked it up. / It felt very heavy. / Probably / it was full of papers. / I handed the envelope / to one of the waiters. / He hurried along the street / after the tourists / and managed to catch them / before they vanished.

(After CP 21)

12

I liked the flat / but there were a few problems. / First of all, / I noticed that the furniture / was rather old, / especially the armchairs /

and one of the tables. / Secondly, the kitchen and the bathroom / needed painting. / Of course / I could do the work myself / but somebody / had to pay for the paint. / However, / I was also worried / about the central heating. / Did it work properly? / It was a big flat / and I felt sure / that it was cold in winter. / I did not want / to use electric fires / because they are expensive.

(After CP 23)

13

Did you hear about Jane? / She got a small part / in a film recently. / She had to ride her bike / to the top of a steep hill / and then go downhill / without stopping. / Unfortunately, / while she was going downhill, / she fell off her bike / into some bushes. / She broke her right arm / and got cuts and bruises / all over. / She was lucky / she didn't break her neck! / Of course the director / was very sorry / but he didn't want this scene / in the film. / So Jane cannot even go / to see herself at the cinema / when she comes out of hospital!

(After CP 25)

14

The other evening / I wanted to get home early / to watch my favourite programme / on TV. / Just as I was leaving, / however, / some students came in to complain / because one of the professors / wanted to cancel a lecture. / They complained steadily / for fifteen minutes. / Then, / as I was driving home, / I noticed / that I was almost out of petrol. / I stopped / at a self-service station / to get some / and arrived home / just in time for my programme. / When I switched on the television, / however, / I found / that it was not working properly. / Luckily, / a friend of mine / has a new video recorder, / so I rang him up / and he recorded the programme / for me.

(After CP 27)

15

The school seemed quite different / as I walked round it. / On the first floor / there were two new laboratories: / one for physics / and one for chemistry. / There were also / several new classrooms. / I could not find / my old classroom, / with its broken windows. / On the way / to the headmaster's study / I passed the library / and the staffroom. / The door of the staffroom / opened as I went past / and I caught a glimpse / of the room inside. / There were teachers reading, / correcting homework / or sitting near the fire. / This at least / was exactly the same!

(After CP 28)

KEY

1 R & d: b)
   B   1b 2c 3b 4a 5a 6b
   C   1 Fred ... Fred and George 2 in the hut 3 the hut
       4 the noise ... George 5 the boys
   D   *Fred:* 1 3 *George*: 2 4 5 6
   E   6 2 9 7 1 10 4 8 3 5
   F   ... found a hut among the trees ... cleaned ... out ... lit a fire ... they had supper ... did not talk much ... they put plenty of wood on the fire ... went to bed ... fell asleep quickly ... watched the flames for a long time ... fell asleep ...

2 R & d: Yes
   B   1b 2a 3b 4a 5b
   C   1 the boat 2 the pilot ... in the lake 3 the 'thing' in the water
       4 in the plane
   D   1 W 2 W 3 R 4 R 5 W 6 W 7 R
   E   3 8 1 6 5 7 2 4
   F   ... they were fishing ... flew over their heads ... was making a strange noise ... they decided to follow the plane ... went down the river in their boat ... they came to a lake ... found the plane in the middle of the lake ... was safe

3 R & d: b)
   B   1b 2c 3a 4c 5c 6c
   C   1 Alan ... Elsa 2 Old Mr Cox ... Alan and Elsa 3 the firemen
   D   1 No 2 No 3 Yes 4 No 5 No 6 Yes 7 No
   E   5 3 10 7 1 9 4 8 2 6
   F   ... went for a walk ... stayed at home ... the newspaper in the front room ... he went to bed ... his newspaper near the electric fire ... the newspaper began to burn ... did not know this ... he was asleep ... smoke came out of the front room window ... the neighbours phoned for the fire engine

4 R & d: 1 did not want 2 glad
   B   1a 2b 3a 4c 5a 6a
   C   1 the tree 2 the woman 3 the roots 4 the hole
       5 found more coins 6 the metal box 7 the things in the box
   D   1 the man 2 the woman 3 the workmen 4 the workmen
       5 the man 6 the man and the woman
   E   1 the man 2 the woman 3 the workmen 4 the woman 5 the man
   F   ... workmen ... apple tree ... yards ... the kitchen window ... cut ... down ... afternoon ... took the roots ... a big hole ... garden ... the hole ... some coins ... a metal box ... jewellery ... got rid of ...

5 R & d: b)
   B   1b 2a 3c 4a 5a 6c 7a 8a
   C   1 Lacey and Barnes ... in the car 2 the garden ... Barnes
       3 in the door 4 the car 5 in their car

D 2 3 4 7 9
E 4 7 2 9 5 6 1 8 3
F ... entered the garden through a small gate ... crept round the side of the garden ... they came to a yard ... told Barnes to wait ... crossed the yard to the kitchen ... got into the house through a small window ... could not open the kitchen door ... called to Barnes ... a car approached the house

6 R & d: b)
B 1b 2c 3a 4a 5c 6c
C 1 the hostel 2 posters 3 at lectures 4 in the corridor
   5 Ann's supervisor 6 the flat 7 Ann's room
D *Ann liked*: 2 4 6 *Ann didn't like*: 1 3 5
E 1 Yes 2 Yes 3 No 4 No 5 No
F ... a hostel ... ugly concrete building ... busy main road ... small ... quite pleasant ... awful ... noisy ... living in a box ... her own age ... share a flat ... an old house ... kitchen ... cook for themselves ... her room ... at the top of the house

7 R & d: b)
B 1a 2a 3c 4a 5b 6c 7b
C *The old man*: 1 2 6
D Places: a village in the Himalayas, outside a restaurant
   Time of day: late evening
   People: a traveller, an old man, a restaurant owner
   Events: an old man tells a traveller about his past
E 2 7 9 4 1 6 10 3 8 5
F ... was sitting at a table outside a restaurant ... came and sat down beside him ... offered to tell the traveller about his future ... asked to hear about his past ... told the traveller about his past ... offered to tell the traveller about his future ... hesitated ... the owner of the restaurant came out ... vanished ... never heard about his future

8 R & d: No
B 1b 2c 3b 4a 5c 6c
C 1 a mine 2 a sailing ship 3 an article 4 a record 5 an orchestra
D 1–c 2–a 3–e 4–b 5–d
E ... sleep well at night ... are tired ... wake up ... dream a lot ... agree ... dreaming is good for you ... relax ... go to sleep ... listen to some music ...

9 R & d: 1 A gorilla 2 In the zoo
B 1a 2a 3b 4c 5a 6b 7a 8c
C 1 on the walls of her bedroom 2 in the shed and garden
   3 in the park 4 to Jane's house 5 to the zoo
D 1W 2R 3R
E 1–c 2–e 3–b 4–a 5–d
F ... gorilla ... from the zoo ... Yes, I have ... In a shed in my garden ... zoo ... van ... park one day ... the gorilla wandering ... lonely ... friends at once ... home

10 **R & d:** 1 landed safely 2 near a farm
   B 1c 2a 3b 4c 5c 6a 7a 8c 9c
   C *Andy*: 2 3 7   *Pete*: 1 4 5 6 8
   D 4 10 8 12 1 6 3 11 9 5 7 2
   E . . . went up into the air . . . waved to Andy and Pete . . . trying to make out landmarks . . . went towards the north . . . to push it towards some mountains in the west . . . Andy and Pete got into some clouds . . . drank some coffee . . . the balloon went over the top of the mountains . . . they came out into the sunlight . . . saw a farm . . . landed . . . invited them to tea

11 **R & d:** 1 Annoyed 2 Because he spoilt their film
   B 1a 2c 3c 4b
   C 1 the canoe 2 his coat 3 the bank 4 the motor boat 5 a blanket 6 a camera
   E Time of day: afternoon
       year: winter
       Places: a motor boat, a bridge, a river
       People: film people, Robert, a boy
       Events: Robert 'saved' a boy. He spoilt a film.
   F . . . winter's afternoon . . . a film . . . a boy . . . canoe . . . the river . . . Help . . . motor boat . . . a bridge . . . dived . . . save . . . him . . . boat . . . pleased . . . a whole afternoon's work

12 **R & d:** 1 His number plate 2 On the road about 15 miles from Marley
   B 1a 2a 3c 4b
   C 1 Alex . . . the views 2 Alex . . . the small green car
       3 Alex . . . his lights 4 Alex . . . at the traffic lights . . . the traffic lights 5 the driver of the green car . . . Alex's window . . . Alex
   E 1–c 2–e 3–b 4–a 5–d
   F . . . was going . . . was . . . enjoying . . . drove very close behind . . . waved . . . drive . . . drove off . . . leaving . . . caught up with . . . got out of . . . tapped . . . fell off . . .

13 **R & d:** c)
   B 1c 2b 3b 4c 5a
   C 1W 2R 3W 4R 5R
   D At the age of three: ran away from home for the first time
       By the age of seven: vanished two or three times a year
       As he grew older: liked to travel on long distance lorries
       At the age of twelve: went to Cairo by plane
       When he left school: joined an expedition to Brazil
   E . . . ran away from home . . . the next village . . . vanish from home two or three times a year . . . quite long distances on foot . . . getting on a bus . . . even a train . . . used to hide on long distance lorries . . . hundreds of miles . . . got on board a plane . . . left school . . . became an explorer

14 R & d: b)
- B 1a 2c 3b 4a
- C 1 the travel agent . . . Mrs Green 2 When they went to Brighton . . . the travel agent . . . Mr and Mrs Green 3 Mrs Green . . . the guidebook . . . the travel agent
- D *The travel agent suggested*: 2 5 *The travel agent didn't suggest*: 1 3 4
  Mrs Green said she wanted: 2 3 5 *Mrs Green said she didn't want*: 1 4
- E . . . get a cheap air ticket to India . . . were very small . . . a family hotel in Brighton . . . were older . . . take our holidays in France : . . our boat tickets . . . grew up . . . cheap holidays in Italy and Spain . . . to go abroad . . . a holiday in Portugal . . . wanted to go to India . . . a two week tour . . . a cheap air ticket . . .

15 R & d: 1 Yes 2 No, but she will probably get one with a friend
- B 1b 2a 3a 4c
- C 1 the people in the street . . . to work 2 the clerk . . . at the Job Centre 3 in her (old) office 4 in a cafe
- D 1 Tues 2 Fri 3 Mon 4 Sun 5 Sat 6 Tues 7 Wed 8 Thurs 9 Mon 10 Fri
- E 1–d 2–a 3–e 4–b 5–c
- F . . . I'm feeling depressed . . . I've lost my job . . . Last Friday . . . Yes . . . been to the Job Centre . . . Not for the moment . . . Good news? Why? . . .

16 R & d: 1 Kay, Nicky, Miss Hunter 2 No
- B 1a 2c 3a 4a
- D 1 Yes 2 Yes 3 Yes 4 No 5 No 6 Yes 7 Yes 8 No
- E Title of book: 'Death comes to the Village'
  Type of book: detective story
  Author: Miss Hunter
  Personal details about author: wore funny clothes, had a large dog, painted
  Nicky's part in the book: postwoman who passes on all the gossip
- F . . . that woman . . . opposite the church . . . Miss Hunter . . . a large dog . . . funny clothes . . . an artist . . . a hobby . . . a writer . . . good friends . . . my next book . . . the village postwoman . . . all the gossip . . . letters . . . very pleased . . .

17 R & d: 1 On the football pools 2 £200,000 3 No
- B 1b 2b 3a 4b
- C 1 a cheque 2 a cup of tea 3 a lorry driver 4 a house 5 a business
- E 6 2 4 9 8 1 5 7 3
- F . . . £200,000 . . . football pools . . . family . . . husband . . . job as a lorry driver . . . house . . . country . . . nice easy life . . . son Ron . . . business . . . computers . . . video . . . daughter Diane . . . cheque . . . charity . . . money . . . share . . . decisions

18 R & d: b)
- B 1c 2b 3a 4c
- C 1 chocolate 2 the (awful) music 3 the rescue van 4 a nice hot drink

E 2 4 5 6 7 9
F ... made a lot of noise ... to keep quiet ... didn't take any notice at all ... fell asleep ... woke him up ... was snoring ... hardly slept at all ... broke down ... to start ... had to send for another one ... change coaches in the rain ... got to Edinburgh ... was so tired ... stayed in bed for the rest of the day ...

19 R & d: He (thought he) saw some flying saucers
B 1a 2a 3b 4c
D 1 in his bedroom 2 in the garden 3 in the field
E 1R 2W 3R 4W 5W 6R
F ... one evening last summer ... getting ready to go to bed ... a low humming noise ... thousands of bees ... my bedroom window ... in the field at the end of the garden ... a number of bright objects coming down ... go to the wall at the end of the garden ... the mysterious objects ... twelve of them in all ... long and thin ... in the centre of the machines ... space suits ... having a meeting ... were from outer space ... to join them ... rushed forward ... pushed me to the ground ... opened my eyes ... was empty ... see any flying saucers ... the happy peaceful planet ...

20 R & d: c)
B 1c 2b 3c 4a 5c
C 1 the man on the bus 2 the man at the bus stop 3 the police inspector 4 Nick
E 1-c 2-b 3-e 4-a 5-d
F ... stood up ... to get off ... found ... was sitting ... think ... was ... felt ... were ... was ... decided ... to hand ... over ... opened ... were ... wanted ... to thank ... had to ... wait ... arrived ...

21 R & d: No
D *The answer isn't in the text*: 2 3 (8: they certainly ate meat and fish!)
E 1 book a table ... hardly ever crowded 2 find a place ... a table in the corner 3 attract the attention ... was busy with the tourists 4 advised his friends about the best dishes 5 very sorry ... no meat or fish left ... offer you an omelette
G ... invited us to one of his favourite restaurants for supper ... it was completely full ... for fifteen minutes ... got a table ... for nearly an hour ... came to our table ... advising us about the best dishes ... went off with our order. He came back ... There's no meat or fish left. All we can offer you is an omelette...

22 R & d: No
D 2 4
E *The answer isn't in the text*: 3 8
F 1 the armchairs ... the big table 2 the central heating doesn't work very well ... the windows don't fit 3 liked the furniture 4 in the flat ... electric fires in winter 5 paint ... paint the bathroom

G 1 armchairs, big table 2 painting the kitchen 3 use electric fires
   4 painting the kitchen
H ... liked it when I moved in ... see it properly ... don't like
   it ... look at the windows ... look at the central heating ... work
   properly ... the kitchen ... paint the bathroom ... we will have to
   leave

23 **R & d:** A fire on board a ship (near Mombasa)
D *The answer isn't in the text*: 6 7 (9: probably yes)
E 1 a small room next to the studio 2 told Ben about the
   programme ... some facts with him 3 Ben did 4 Ben's
   book ... find a copy 5 the fire (on board ship) ... be on the boat
   at the same time
F *The interviewer*: 2 3 4 *Ben*: 1 5. The order is 4 2 5 1 3
G ... a writer ... wrote a book ... a steward on one of the boats that
   went between England and Australia ... tourists and
   immigrants ... caught fire ... we were on the boat too ... the one
   exciting thing that happened during the voyage ... a copy of the
   book ... get hold of ...

24 **R & d:** 1 She was a shopkeeper 2 No
D *The answer isn't in the text*: 3 4 9
E 1 has to travel twenty miles or more ... a cinema in our town
   2 the screen is too small ... she likes going to the cinema
   3 be an actress ... used to wait outside film studios 4 a very
   small part ... rehearsed 5 took all her friends ... she wasn't
F ... started to make a film ... get a part in it ... the director is
   going to be there ... met the director ... offered me a role in the
   film ... have a small part ... rehearsed ... has helped ... turned
   the sitting room ... was marvellous ... congratulated me ... is the
   beginning of my film career ...

25 **R & d:** She fell off her bike
D *The answer isn't in the text*: 3 (though probably a week) 4
E 1 in a small house ... sixty miles 2 going for a long walk ... a bike
   3 the hill was very steep ... get off the bike
   4 the brakes did not work 5 began to work ... shot off the bike
G She went to stay in a small house in the hills about sixty miles from
   Montreal. It was a very isolated place. She got up early the following
   morning because she intended to go for a long walk. Instead she went
   for a ride on an old bike. Well, after about ten miles she came to a
   steep hill and, as she was going downhill, she found the brakes didn't
   work. She kept on trying them and when they suddenly did begin to
   work, she shot off her bike into some bushes! She broke her left arm
   and injured her shoulder, and now she's in hospital in Montreal.

26 **R & d:** 1 *Travel with us* 2 No (hardly any of it)
D *The answer isn't in the text*: 2 3 8
E 1 favourite programme ... Friday evening ... six o'clock 2 rang up
   to complain ... leave the office early 3 ages to get ... got home
   4 watching the programme ... rang 5 go round and pay for his petrol

F 1 *Travel with us* 2 the garage 3 People forget to pay
G . . . a customer rang up to complain just as I was leaving . . . I noticed that I needed petrol, so I had to stop at one of those self-service petrol stations to get some. The pump wasn't working very well, so that took ages . . . the phone rang. It was the man from the garage. 'You forgot to pay for your petrol!' he informed me. . .

27 R & d: 1 A meeting and the lecture room 2 She recorded her lecture
C 1 the phone 2 the meeting 3 her lecture 4 the cassette recorder 5 her voice
D *The answer isn't in the text*: 5 6 9 15
F 1 the meeting was at eleven 2 Dr Allen to cancel her lecture 3 had a new cassette recorder 4 switched on the cassette recorder 5 students there . . . cassette recorders
G . . . that she wouldn't be able to give her lecture because she had an important meeting . . . she never cancels lectures . . . I've recorded my lecture on this cassette recorder, so you'll be able to listen to my lecture while I go to the meeting. So I'll be in two places at once! . . . she switched on the cassette recorder and left . . . switched on ours and went off for coffee

28 R & d: To inspect it

D	Tandem	went	across	the school yard
			along	the corridor
			into	the headmaster's study
			past	the staffroom his old classroom the library
		didn't go	into	the staffroom his old classroom the library any of the classrooms

E *The answer isn't in the text*: 4 8
F 1 paused in the yard 2 of the staffroom . . . some teachers inside 3 a bell rang and the corridor was full of noisy boys
4 the headmaster's study . . . Come in 5 has ever come back to inspect the school
G I went back to my old school today. It was my first visit there for twenty years and of course it was a very strange experience. First of all I walked round the school and it seemed much the same except for three new laboratories. Then I went and stood outside my old classroom. There was plenty of noise inside (as usual!). I stood outside the library too: there were boys inside, all working quietly. But then suddenly everything changed! A bell rang and the corridor was full of noisy boys! I was glad when I finally got to the headmaster's study!

29   **R & d:** 1 His watch   2 Yes
     D   *The answer isn't in the text*: 8 11 (although it probably was dirty)
     E   1 a long open one   2 people passing up and down, a visit from the ticket collector   3 he came from the restaurant car   4 he couldn't find his watch
     F   1 an hour or so . . . put away his papers   2 the ticket collector . . . came to look at their tickets   3 my watch is in that plastic bag   4 among the plastic coffee cups, half-eaten biscuits and pieces of paper   5 a cup of coffee . . . the restaurant car was closed
     G   . . . did some work for about an hour. Then, as he began to put away his papers, Mark asked me what the time was. I started to look for my watch – I thought it was on the table – but I couldn't find it anywhere. It was really very odd, because I remembered putting it on the table. But then Mark remembered seeing a man with a big plastic bag, who cleared away the coffee cups. Someone said the man came from the restaurant car, so I went along and explained my problem. At first the man didn't want to empty out the plastic bag but he agreed in the end when I explained that my watch was very valuable. And of course my watch *was* there – among all the plastic coffee cups, half-eaten biscuits and pieces of paper!

30   **R & d:** It had a hole near one of the pockets
     D   *The answer isn't in the text*: 3 6
     E   1 to get them into the wardrobe   2 hardly ever wore . . . never wore at all   3 mend the hole . . . along with the other clothes   4 Can I come and see you   5 tried to mend the hole (with the wrong colour cotton)
     F   1 clothes (suits etc)   2 ones he wore a lot, ones he hardly ever wore, ones he never wore   3 cars, computers, art, sport, latest films, most recent books
     G   . . . my friend Dennis to see my brother Dick . . . didn't like Dennis . . . cars and computers, art and sport, the latest films and the most recent books . . . looking at Dennis . . . remember something . . . Dennis' jacket . . . in a secondhand clothes shop . . . there was a hole near one of the pockets which some fool tried to mend with the wrong colour cotton . . . it was Dick's jacket – and he was the person who tried to mend the hole with wrong colour cotton